POEMS 1975–1995

Micheal O'Siadhail was born in 1947. He was educated at Clongowes Wood College, Trinity College Dublin, and the University of Oslo. A full-time writer, he has published nine collections of poetry. He was awarded an Irish American Cultural Institute prize for poetry in 1982, and the Marten Toonder Prize for Literature in 1998. His poem suites, *The Naked Flame*, *Summerfest* and *Crosslight* were commissioned and set to music for performance and broadcasting.

His latest collection is *Our Double Time* (Bloodaxe Books, 1998). *Hail! Madam Jazz: New and Selected Poems* (Bloodaxe Books, 1992) includes selections from six of his collections, *The Leap Year* (1978), *Rungs of Time* (1980), *Belonging* (1982), *Springnight* (1983), *The Image Wheel* (1985), as well as the whole of *The Chosen Garden* (1990) and a new collection *The Middle Voice* (1992). A new selection of his earlier poetry, *Poems 1975-1995*, drawing on both *Hail! Madam Jazz* and his later collection *A Fragile City* (Bloodaxe Books, 1995), was published by Bloodaxe in 1999.

He has given poetry readings and broadcast extensively in Ireland, Britain, Europe and North America. In 1985 he was invited to give the Vernam Hull Lecture at Harvard and the Trumbull Lecture at Yale University. He represented Ireland at the Poetry Society's European Poetry Festival in London in 1981. He was writer-in-residence at the Yeats Summer School in 1991.

He has been a lecturer at Trinity College Dublin and a professor at the Dublin Institute for Advanced Studies. Among his many academic works are *Learning Irish* (Yale University Press, 1988) and *Modern Irish* (Cambridge University Press, 1989). He was a member of the Arts Council of the Republic of Ireland (1988-93) and of the Advisory Committee on Cultural Relations (1989-97), a founder member of Aosdána (Academy of distinguished Irish artists) and a former editor of *Poetry Ireland Review*. He is the founding chairman of ILE (Ireland Literature Exchange), and was a judge for *The Irish Times* ESB 1998 Theatre Awards and the 1998 *Sunday Tribune*/Hennessy Cognac Literary Awards.

Micheal O'Siadhail

POEMS
1975-1995

HAIL! MADAM JAZZ ◆ A FRAGILE CITY

BLODAXE BOOKS

ISBN: 1 85224 495 X

First published 1999 by
Bloodaxe Books Ltd,
P.O. Box 1SN,
Newcastle upon Tyne NE99 1SN.

Bloodaxe Books Ltd acknowledges
the financial assistance of Northern Arts.

Cover printing by J. Thomson Colour Printers Ltd, Glasgow.

Printed in Great Britain by
Cromwell Press Ltd, Trowbridge, Wiltshire.

For Bríd

ACKNOWLEDGEMENTS

This book reprints the whole of *Hail! Madam Jazz: New & Selected Poems* (Bloodaxe Books, 1992) and *A Fragile City* (Bloodaxe Books, 1995). *Hail! Madam Jazz* was drawn from Micheal O'Siadhail's six previous collections: from *The Leap Year* (1978), *Rungs of Time* (1980), *Belonging* (1982) – versions of poems originally published as *An Bhliain Bhisigh*, *Runga* and *Cumann* by An Clóchomhar – and from *Springnight* (Bluett 1983), *The Image Wheel* (Bluett 1985) and *The Chosen Garden* (The Dedalus Press 1990), which appears in its entirety, with two additional poems not included in the first edition.

For the poems from *Hail! Madam Jazz* appearing in the third section, *Belonging*, and for the new poems in the seventh section, *The Middle Voice*, acknowledgements are due to the editors of *The Decision Maker*, *Rhinoceros*, *Stet*, *Poetry Ireland Review*, *Poets for Africa* (1986), *Christmas in Ireland* (Mercier, 1990), *The Flowering Tree* (Wolfhound Press 1991); to the University of Wisconsin-Milwaukee, and RTE Radio, who commissioned a number of these poems for the song cycles *The Naked Flame* (1988, with Seoirse Bodley) and *Summerfest* (1992).

For *A Fragile City*, acknowledgements are due to the editors of these publications in which some of those poems first appeared: *Chapman*, *Christmas in Ireland* (Mercier Press, 1985), *Gown*, *Irish Times*, *Krino*, *London Magazine*, *Orbis*, *Oxford Poetry*, *Poetry Book Society Anthology 2* (PBS/Hutchinson, 1991), *Poetry Durham*, *Poetry Ireland Review*, *Rhinoceros*, *Stand* and *Stet*; and to RTE Radio and WBEZ, Chicago where a number of the poems were broadcast.

The first three epigraphs to *A Fragile City* are from the following editions: *Selected Poems of Rainer Maria Rilke*, translated by Robert Bly (Harper & Row, 1981); *Selected Writings* by Mirjam Tuominen, translated by David McDuff (Bloodaxe Books, 1994); and *Complete Poems* by Karin Boye, translated by David McDuff (Bloodaxe Books, 1994).

CONTENTS

THE CHOSEN GARDEN (1990)

I. *Departure*

II. *A Blurred Music*

III. *Fists of Stone*

IV. *Turns and Returns*

A Fragile City (1995)

FILTERED LIGHT

VEILS AND MASKS

Introduction: *Miss Unfathomable*

I was a late starter. I was 28 before I really got down to it. Yet I had only ever wanted to make poems. I think I was confused – or was the world confused? Or both? Maybe each generation imagines it grows up at a time when everything starts to change. Sigrid Undset, the great Norwegian novelist, was probably right in believing that the human heart doesn't change much over thousands of years. I'm sure it's a constellation of temperament and childhood's experience that drives any poet towards words. Yet, like climates, the spiritual and intellectual ambience does slowly change. I certainly have always had the feeling that I'm living my life at a watershed.

It's almost as if the rigid boundaries and the excesses of Modernity gradually espoused by Europe in its fright after the Thirty Years' War three centuries earlier had come home to roost. Two world wars of nations during another three decades. Born two years after it ended, I suppose I have been attempting, at each stage of my fifty odd years, both to cope with my own temperament and to search for meaning against the backdrop of a world rearranging and repairing itself.

The 1950s, in suburban Dublin at any rate, were a settled and timid time of recovery. A childhood where everything was steady in the heavens. The piano was in the sitting-room and it seemed Chopin was still sounding a hundred years after his death in Paris. Even boarding school had hardly altered since Joyce fixed it in *A Portrait of the Artist as a Young Man*. Then, we burst out into the 1960s. There was a raucous prosperity, the television replaced the piano, a huge surge of freedom as we broke the taboos and, socialists all, lived our Bohemian student life. At Trinity College where I was a student, it was fashionable to talk of existentialism, the philosophies of Sartre and Camus. The ideas of Marx, Nietzsche and Freud, postponed by the wars, were now generally in the air. Beckett's *Waiting for Godot* seemed to have caught the mood. We were all angry young men and women and read those paperbacks about sociology and psychology, and we felt we knew what lay hidden behind everything.

For many of us there was a tristesse about the 1970s, a let-down as life settled into its ordinariness. Many glimpsed the abyss and peered over its edge. I recall in those years I often walked and sat in St Stephen's Green in Dublin, a stone's throw from where I was born. For all the terror of our century, for all our angst and knowingness, just wandering there watching ducks in a pond and the listening to the gossip and laughter of people as they passed, the world seemed sweet and new. There were tiny glances of infinity. And slowly I gave into the wonder of the world. All I needed to do was to dare, to tauten towards the light like a sunflower. I was 26 and this would be my 'leap year'.

Anyhow I dared. And it seemed as if life began to expand. I wanted to seize just one of those glances of infinity. I wanted to tell the world. Strangely, the wonder keeps eluding me and yet I always believe the next poem will refract a little more. So a universe which might have narrowed became now an endless jazz improvisation. Madam Jazz had made me her own. I heard her joys and grievings. The collections began to appear. The first three: *The Leap Year, Rungs of Time* and *Belonging* I wrote originally in Irish. After that, feeling the need to speak to those who shared with me an English-speaking upbringing, I always wrote in English. English literature had been my first love. Then, came *Springnight* and *The Image Wheel*.

I'd spent the opening few years of the 1970s as a lecturer at Trinity College Dublin, but I'd left as I knew teaching wasn't for me. I enjoyed it but knew it would exhaust me. I was invited to join the staff of the Dublin Institute for Advanced Studies. There I'd stay for 13 years until I left to devote my life entirely to poetry. The mixture of writing and linguistic research was more congenial. But in the end, I didn't want to divide my energies any more. The quality of concentration I could then afford made me move from collections united by an angle of vision to books with an architecture, an overriding focus. It took me five years to complete *The Chosen Garden*. It was an effort to face my own journey, to comprehend and trace one's own tiny epic: setting out, challenging the world, ordeal and failure, the underworld, achievement, the delight of return and re-rooting to open to the world in a new way. A journey from the garden chosen for me by my parents, through boarding school, youthful excesses, ideologies, despair, learning to love and reconnect with society, to the garden I'd chosen for myself.

Temperament again, I suppose, but I've always relished poetry that comes from the core, that's written in blood. Again the climate was shifting subtly. Messieurs Derrida, Foucault and de Man had percolated through and deconstructionism was in the air. The flight into irony wasn't for me. Even extreme Modernism seemed to be less a solution than an extension of the Romantic escape into self. No, there must never again be one overarching and commanding viewpoint. Yet I think my instinctive humanist reaction was that beyond self was a community, beyond the individual endeavour a tradition, and beyond Cartesian radical doubt a trust. Beauty and truth are somehow in dialogue with a particular community which attempts in its joys and sufferings, its successes and mistakes, its ecstasy and incompleteness to keep itself in good repair. Are poets in the business of repair? Invisible menders?

In 1989 the Berlin Wall came tumbling down, yet another move in the recovery from world wars. I was hatching a new series of poems, *The Middle Voice*. My mind was turning to tradition, that sense of being a voice in the middle between a generation fading out and one coming behind and into it's own. I also loved the resonances of the title: a grammatical voice somewhere between activity and passivity, a melodic line weaving across the centre of a part-song.

Gradually, I became fascinated by trust. It seemed to be the oil and hinge of our world. A third of humankind lives in conurbations, so that McLuhan's image of the global village with its sense of relationship and intimacy rings false. I wanted to capture the frailty of trust which underpins the *polis* and tumbled to the image of *A Fragile City*. It became a meditation on the appeal of every human for caring, on how because of race, gender or wealth we so often veil and mask the other's call. I wanted to muse on how even in trust, like children playing hopscotch, we both need our boundaries and need to transcend them. Even in quantum theory, there are boundaries; as Heisenberg has taught us, certainty in the measurement of a sub-atomic particle's position and momentum can be mutually exclusive. It seemed to me that only by trust can the rifts between head and heart heal. Hospitality is a boundary-crossing that affords us the trust to take time out, to feast and dance.

But we're all part of a tradition. I still have tucked away from my primary school four pages of *Poets and Poetry for Irish Schools (Senior Book)*. There they are: Robert Herrick's 'To Daffodils', Patrick H. Pearse's 'The Wayfarer', William Collins's 'How Slept the Brave', Thomas Hood's 'Past and Present', and Alfred, Lord Tennyson's 'Crossing the Bar'. Looking at these tattered pages now, I notice the wistful mood of the anthologist. I remember as a schoolboy how they filled me with peculiar tears, half delight and half a strange boundless desire. A moment becomes a touchstone and a life is shaped. I still relish the *allegro* quality of Herrick's love poems. Then, I tend towards the earlier periods. I delight in the clearheaded jewel-and-poison excitement of the Elizabethans

Jonson, Raleigh (for all the havoc he wrought in my country), in beloved, endless Shakespeare and in the complex thought and play of the Jacobeans Herbert and Donne. There again, I love Hopkins, Frost, Auden and Kavanagh. And where does that leave all the living writers both older and contemporary that I admire and draw constant sustenance from? Such a tradition. Such a privilege to spend a life in this community.

What of the wider world of poetry? I've had the good fortune to visit other linguistic traditions. All leave their trace. There's the risk of cultural name-dropping but not to allude to some of them seems a sort of treason. I relish the outburst of Early Irish nature poetry and the raw passion of the Irish folk love poetry. The Scandinavian tradition from the beautiful gnomic Edda to the Norwegians Gunnar Reiss-Andersen, Herman Wildenvey, Einar Skjæraasen and Halldis Moren Vesaas alongside the Swedes Dan Anderson and Karin Boye all cut deep into my youth. I love Rilke's extraordinary ripe and dense formality and the peculiar magic of Paul Valéry. Then there's Dante. What of the classics, Homer, Catullus and Virgil? And there are so many worlds of poetry beyond my orbit. Of course I'm also nourished by novels and plays. What of all the other streams – of music, painting, science, philosophy, politics, sport – which feed into the tradition? It seems we're tapping into something huge and opulent.

Maybe it's this unlimited richness that makes poetry a lifetime's pursuit. We never can arrive. Madam Jazz, that femme fatale, is never to be caught:

> *O Minx beyond this mind's embrace*
> *Hider-Go-Seeker, Miss Unfathomable*
> *Demurring Lady playing at the chase.*

I start and start and start again.

MICHEAL O'SIADHAIL

Hail! Madam Jazz

NEW & SELECTED POEMS

(1992)

HAIL! MADAM JAZZ

Worship, hold her a moment in thought.
Femme fatale, she shapes another face,
unveils an idol. O Never-To-Be-Caught,

O Minx beyond this mind's embrace,
Hider-Go-Seeker, Miss Unfathomable,
Demurring Lady playing at the chase.

As stars or atoms we turn, fall
towards each other's gravity. I spin
in your love's nexus, Mistress All.

Once a child of Newton's fallen
apple, I'd the measure of your ways.
My stars, my atoms, are we one?

Mischievous Strategy, Madam Jazz!
Old tunes die in metamorphosis.
Rise, fall, reawakening. I praise.

FROM **THE LEAP YEAR**
(1978)

Sunflower

The danger of tautening towards the sun:
To lose is to lose all.
Too much gravity and I'm undone;
If I bend, I fall.

Tell me it's all worth this venture,
Just the slightest reassurance,
And I'll open a bloom, I'll flower
At every chance.

Then praise me all the way to the sky,
Praise me with light, lover,
Oh, praise me, praise me, praise me
And I live forever.

The Bridge

For years I puzzled over those words of the Curé d'Ars
About that Frenchman who threw himself into the water,
He'd said in the moments between the bridge and river
A man prepares his soul.

For years I couldn't understand his strange pilgrimage
Until I too had walked to the edge of that bridge
And there staring into the dark had caught a glimpse
Of light in the bridge's eye.

For years I puzzled over those words of the Curé d'Ars.
We accept, he said, even what an ill-wind has blown.
In that space between the arch and the river's foam
Am I made whole?

Of Course

Of course, it's only reasonable:
This journey was incomprehensible,
At every glance's end, winter waited.

But today I saw the spring, my friend.
A whole wide world has germinated.
Hail and welcome!

Just today winter flung off its coat
And humbly stood outside the womb
Begging again a world without end.

Compliment

Were those women meek and humble
Who once whispered in a man's ear
That a god was a dominant male?
Then tell me that we know better.

Among the bright women of the world
There have always been those goddesses,
As we crossed our makeshift scaffold,
A universe built in time and space.

Did some of these women think it through,
That few who drifted through my youth;
The two or three, who somehow drew
My threads together, wove my cloth?

A wonderful cloth, my shirt of linen,
My chequered gift, a self they've woven,
This shirt that's closer than the bone,
The bright women of my world have given.

Graffiti

The warmest summer in a hundred years;
The toughest work, the sweetest wine;
As usual the women were even finer
Than ever before.

This was the summer I at last conceded
The unfathomables, even pleasures I'd miss.
Was this ageing or a glimpse of paradise
Through the needle's eye?

Like the monk who chronicled a dread of wintery
Vikings, I felt the need to mention
One good season. For the annals my entry:
This was summer.

Temptation

In this park, lead us not into temptation.
Does an evil angel walk in Stephen's Green?

'Please, just good sense,' he says respectfully,
'I plead with you to stop all this immediately.

'Who'd mind but look at those old women feeding
Ducks. And, friend, that's where you're heading.'

Then after a billion years of pure anticipation,
That moment, especially for me, the sun had risen.

There and then, I knew them by their beauty
Those three eternal goddesses of our story,

Bending to feast a world of ducks on a crust.
Do they weave for us our threads of fate from dust?

Regrets

When March first came in, I'd thought
I'd concentrate on nothing but my tree;
Slowly as a child, slowly so slowly,

It would germinate, shoot by shoot.
Talk of a war, a worry, a distraction;
Then, one small thing after another
Somehow smudged my best intention,
Drawing me from the business of a father.

Now, over again the need for autumn,
For three secret seasons in the womb
Before I'm born to re-attend my tree's
Slow, precise unfolding of a history.

Dispossessed

At a rally, standing on a bench, I saw that woman;
A heart on her sleeve seemed to flinch as she began:

'Don't tell me it's over, we're an extinct breed,
The hand that planted lives, the tree is dead.

I'm resolved to save those leaves, come what may,
If it means I'll be nailed onto this passion tree.'

I once saw a woman standing on a park bench
Gluing a yellowed leaf back onto a branch.

Was the tree stretching down a naked limb,
Lifting that woman quietly up into its bosom,

To cradle her gently, then rock and soothe her,
Tucking her into a long sweet sleep of winter?

Season

A season ago these trees had flung a libraryful
Of ochre leaflets in a crosswind's free-for-all,

As if determined to pose for months in the nude,
To allow the low sun warm their leafless blood.

And still it's winter. Still this twentieth century.
What news item will we run today? What's the story

To break? The naked trees, a bird's plaintive sound
Asking whether a world still breathes underground.

The hard-crusted soil turns in its sleep and cries:
'Just live, man, I'm busy pushing up the daisies.'

Something young and dangerous stirs in the marrowbone
Of earth. Await the leap and resurrection of a season.

FROM **RUNGS OF TIME**

(1980)

Sand

Time is sand
On a river's bed,
Beyond blustering men
Boast and whistle;
Over here women whisper,
Their silk skirts rustle
Across the water.

Such unfathomable understanding,
a well that can't be sounded,
until the sloe will bloom white,
and yesterday returns.

Woman's will to love
is a well of abundance;
a waterlily on its surface,
the shallow share of a male.

We tried to sound it once
but were far too selfish,
we saw our own poor reflection –
the well itself is bottomless.

Time is sand
In a lover's mind;
Age and childhood recycle,
Form and substance are one;
The world is a youth again
And sand is time.

Roofing

A livelong day, a night's secrecies:
Only the rafters themselves must know
The beams' strains and stresses, slow
Givings and takings, the touch and go
Of our attunements and compromise, how
We raise the roof or make our peace.

A timber's head nestles in another's,
A mitred joint, this bevelled match,
Two beams and their collar-beam which
Shape a triangle, the tie and apex
Of togetherness. So easily one forgets
Couples are a liaison of two rafters.

And always under us or in between
That dangerous breach we never close,
A zone for household gods we choose
Or need. Here, then, allow some room
For unlike memories, dreams to dream,
A living space for a separate passion.

A roof is framing our slanted intimacy.
Unless each of these matching couples
Beds snugly down into opposite walls,
The timbers sag. Somehow we're stronger
In separateness; this sloping encounter
Our braced ridge, our tie of ecstasy.

Circus Rider

Astride two loping haltered horses
He circles the arena, a *tour de force*
Astraddle a skittish gap. Watch him
Holding those barebacks in tandem.

A deft balance. They seem to want
To veer apart as though two different
Voices called. We clap to the music;
A rhythm curbs the tension of his risk.

'Please more rope,' begs a right hand,
'Allow your nature the scope and bond
Of its affections. Don't rein me in.
I'm the cry of your children's children.'

'Stay the course!' whispers a left hand,
'It doesn't matter what others demand,
I'm your ecstasy, queen single-mindedness
Chafing a dream with pure-bred giddiness.'

At last the rider's moment of applause,
A smiling lap in his red striped blouse
Astride our joy and wonder. Who'd remember
All the halter's sweated fray and tear?

Work

You insatiable bitch you!
even still I can't quit you
never flit from your manger.

Again and again, you slut,
so cruelly you've looted
my meagre legacy of years.

You're the merciless whore,
a wantonness still scourging me,
agony of desire in the loin

I'll never want to do without.
Rather you than your counterpart:
a tediousness turning all to dust.

You're the ghost of an old lover,
you there at my bed's four corners;
even sweetness palls without you.

An Oslo Brewery

Seven a.m. sharp. Right on the button
electric life is recreated. A shuddering
back into action of greased and sleepy
machinery. The steam whinges and rises.
A first arrival from the locker dodges
past iron girders, climbs to his post.
A clang and blare loudens. It's hell
for leather. A conveyer shakes a *joie
de vivre*, a huge quaking expectancy,
a world in suspense awaits its morning's
bottles. A quarter of an hour. Hurry!
Stack up those labels, snug and ready,
give those containers a fix of glue.
A move on, mate! A gooey bucket tilts
and spills. Someone swears. A messer!
A few minutes yet. The rush and pitch,
rattle of fellowship and tempered steel,
camaraderie of cog for tooth. Solidarity.
The steam clouds the ceiling's lights
blotting out the dome of work's temple.
Every mother's son and daughter bends,
priming, tuning, fixing, bringing a house
to order. The daily advent of the bottle.

And there she goes. A first bottle
up to its neck in ale. Thousands more
behind, driven by their gods, urgent,
relentless, skittling onto the conveyor,
hiss and jostle for position on the belt.
Clack and rat-a-tat, rattle and whirr.
For every bottle the cap that fits.
Clack and rat-a-tat, rattle and whirr.
Two labels per bottle, belly and neck.
Clack and rat-a-tat, rattle and whirr.
A brand for every bottle, a personality;
for every bottle its body and soul,
as it squeezes towards the carton machine
tended by its acolyte labellers and packers.
And still seven endless hours to go.

How else can all this time be thought of?
Electric light doesn't rise or set,
heavens don't fill and darken with rain,
no chance break to shelter in a ditch.
Still seven hours of wilderness to go.
Imagine a taskmaster, any pleasured sultan
measured or ruthless as the clock's dial
putting such a face on inner intensities,
a holy of holies of crystal oscillations.
Clack and rat-a-tat, rattle and whirr.
Well, what time do you reckon it's now?
Numb slowly, fall into a day's reverie.

Look out! Numbskull. Nitwit. *Tosk!*
A bottle trips, stumbles along the belt
unlabelled. Droves of bottles fumble
one another, climb and jam in clusters.
For God's sake, stop that conveyor!
A stupid idiot. And it's time lost!
Remember the bonus. A sudden squabbling.
Recall the creed. A Serb is taking off
gloves to wipe his forehead and dream
a fortnight at home. He smiles his motto:
The more bottles, the more money.

Outside a day is lengthening in its sky.
These bottles live out their inner life
by time and motion, a sacred predestination
from top to label, to pack and fork-lift.
A loud whoosh! Some newly-filled bottle
collides and bursts. And nobody startles
or heeds a blow-out. Half-asleep, half-awake.
A Turk is relighting his cigarette butt;
a packer pulls her rubber apron tighter,
stooping that grey and wasting chassis.
The more bottles, the more our money.
Read here a winding litany of unlanced
heart-sores, a long sigh of forbearance.
Something will never find itself in words.
The more bottles, the more our bonus.

According to the Act: so-so many minutes
break per hour allowed for self-repair.
Somebody is sitting on an upturned crate,
a mind is ungearing itself into neutral.
Closeted in the john, an ochre skinned
addict swills a lukewarm beer on the sly.
A young bearded radical preaches the day
when every inhuman clock is torn down,
but his dream is a nightmare even stranger
than the daily abyss of clocked up hours.
'Is this then the inferno?' his youth asks.
Across the belt Turkish women joke and laugh.
A world always hung between a hell and heaven.

So slowly the time is stealing forward.
How is it certain this day has happened?
Who arrives in dark, leaves in dark.
Lowry's brittle figures ashen and pink
File to the exit. Press the random button.
Red: frisk for any smuggled bottles,
Green: pass unsearched through the gate.
'A good weekend,' someone says, 'And you too.'
Behind the red bulb's buzzer sounds. Frames
veer into the street. A strange inalienable
dignity flushes those sombre homing faces.

Affliction

More than the pain, the anticipation,
That long anxiety before the travail.
Is suffering this low November sun
Slanting a mean and narrowed angle,
A subtle stinging glint of affliction
Touching this face against my will?
Caress me. Even a hint of solace.
Oh, empty then the fullest chalice.

More than the affliction, the aftermath.
The will indulged or the will checked
Are beams of a cross, a length and breath
Where desire and fragility intersect.
Can patience heal or must the sun
Hoist again my light? Or is it both,
Process and outcome kneaded into one?
My heart struggles with a crux of growth.

Friendship

No wonder we're happy just to meet,
As the spirit moves us, on and off;
An easy rapport of nothing to prove
As we unwind, stretch in the light of
Each other's sun.

Little wonder we're content to meet
Once in a while, just as it suits.
Such concurrence never frets or doubts;
We've shot our long wedge-shaped roots
To the water plane.

No wonder a fluid runs from root
To root, a conduit of *eau de vie*,
An underground, our liquid conspiracy
The cherishings and waterings of intimacy
For a feast or drought.

Definition

Father my own, what should I say to you?
There was father after father after you,
As many fathers as a youth shed skins.

Good father, by stealth you seemed to fix
My boundaries. *Alter ego*, yardstick,
Needle's eye I pass through into a world.

Is a shell defined by its need to unshell?
A subtle fragility, breakthrough and bustle,
A scurrying from one prototype to another,

Doubt after doubt unhusking to the kernel.
At last, this ease between modelled and model.
Father, comrade, what should I say to you?

The Umbrella

Again he overtakes me. Who is that fellow
Stepping out past me along a morning street,
So polished, so clean-shaven, dapper and fit,
A single stride behind his furled umbrella?

I know I've sometimes felt, as he outpaced me,
a knife of envy. Am I too diffident or callow?
My Bohemian soul covets such swish authority,
A sureness striding behind a furled umbrella.

But is it a calm and genial walking stick?
I see a crop lashing a haunch in its sweat,
A baton with an orchestra breathing its beat,
A cane poised to thrash or hold in check.

But that tie! I recognise an old school emblem.
It might well be his seat was once worn thin
By a bench that years later left a countersign
In mine as I fidget *Ad Majorem Dei Gloriam*.

I glimpse his face through a childhood's lens.
What's a furled umbrella so anxious to swat?
Today as he passed, I wondered if we'd caught
A giddiness flickering in each other's glance.

A Birthday

Already that's one year you have on Schubert,
A whole year to bloom before Christ's torture.

Strange how after a frantic decade of imprudence,
These thirties seem almost nearer to our teens.

Is this gravity at last bending us to its rule
Or a fertile ring of history turned in the skull?

Is it age the thief plotting against our will
Or an auxiliary circle curved within a circle?

A cock kicking the wind, determined to fight;
Another light-year moving towards the infinite?

Then tell me first which pure truth is truer –
Riddle me that today, my wise old codger!

Becoming

What's infinite and female in a circle
Eludes me. Always that hub of room,
A roundedness arcing beyond the angle
Of my vision. I'm yearning at the rim.

A juttedness seems to fawn and dither,
The moth of my desire angling at every
Candle butt that flickers a come-hither,
A fickleness roving near the periphery.

Ah, women. Insiders, bearers of the womb
That shaped us, it's as though you dwell
Within a turning, somehow always at home
And there beyond me, your being a circle.

Whatever's in a ring can never arrive
Just keeps on bringing its curve full
Circle, a figure certain and receptive.
This eternal becoming, this making whole.

FROM **BELONGING**

(1982)

Approach

Almost familiar but still vigilant,
we zigzag. A gentle dig, a careful hint.
We watch the other's words. Will or won't?
A child once burnt will dread a fire,
a terror nestle deep in the flesh.
Come a storm, will we recall fair weather?

Will I, won't I? We soften each other up
with floods of talk. Now warily we swap
old secrecies. And is there no end
to all we share? Years of one temperament
have plotted for us a common pilgrimage,
shaping us into each other's image.

Anxious still, we're probing one another.
Oh, let's not waste this precious time.
I won't mince words. You're my brother!
I will. I yield. Manoeuvre as you like.
Without you – I'm alone, bare-shouldered.
A friendship thickens water into blood.

Nest

Marvel at the work of this nest:
love-straws kneaded into kin;
still the nest's law is to scatter
feather and wing, one and all.

We're born to betray the nest,
to quit the brood, flutter alone:
brothers no longer of a feather,
sisters already lone travellers.

And so it is. In spite of ourselves,
no sooner now the tribe together
than all the nestling sores lurk,
we're rivals in the peck and chatter.

Star-guided or even by chance,
blank strangers gathered this nest;
its fragility still its own fail-safe:
daring to gather is daring to scatter.

Forebear

Delia Garvan, it's you I accuse.
The deck stacked, I was dealt
a five of trumps, a flighty hand.

You're to blame for the wild abandon;
at your door my Connacht contrariness,
aceless robber of insanity's trump.

In the throes of the game you snapped,
broke our mind's lobsided bargain
between frail wisdoms and a giddiness,

threw in your hand. And still traces
of your deranged years whisper
conspiracy, hide in genes of my game.

Yet it's you I always have to thank:
madness and song are the same suit.
I praise your name. I play your trump.

Temperament

Morning. Into seething water
oatmeal thrown anew
to dance the whirlpool.
All eagerness, tending it
I watch again creation.

Damn my consuming fire!
A gift or a derangement?
Taut as a fiddle's bow,
anxiety hardens my veins.

Come now, why the panic?
Unless a day is spent to the full,
unless a moment catches courage,
all is a duck's trace in water.

Half-eternity at least, it's said,
to aim at the target, another
half-eternity to be nonchalant
the instant the arrow is fired.

Damn this endless ardour!
My cravings are a millstone.
Under the sway of some urge,
I burn on a griddle of fervour.

The oatmeal spins a storm.
A million granules rise;
fuddling, whizzing, rivalling
truths. What's to be done?
Patience. Wait for the thickening.

Salute

So tell me how are things going?
But I hear a stranger's unconcern
lurk in syllables of our greeting.

I've no regrets. Why should I?
What seems best was done;
once that way, this way now.

Still such easy greetings don't fit.
This trivial chatter on a street
could broach our memory's cache.

Doesn't it now seem bizarre
that we're more than strangers,
as if old intimacies come between us?

But watch my eye for the clue.
Neither of us has grounds to rue
that our purposes once crossed.

No, not regret, more a chagrin
that a street's chance salute contains
all of what was once affection.

Aside

For all the years we've spent together,
again I want to summon a self aside
to mull over that falling for you,
gather up an image of this double-life.

In some haze of workaday mystery
we're ferried across the abyss;
drop by drop our time elopes
and still I can't trap its image.

I've no sooner focused a memory,
no sooner fixed a picture of you,
than you flee the frame I've managed,
a fluid image drifts away from me.

Somehow a glimpse is never more
than a plan by which we manoeuvre;
do I imagine some distant eternity,
a skylight onto a travelling image?

From the daily dream of your company
(sunny water running over shingle)
this is my yearly summons aside,
an overview of all that's between us.

Waiting

Under the meagrest of sparks
a random blast of wind
turns fuel to fire.

In every game one tough move,
a startling turn from underdog
to a winning upper hand.

Intimacy and a split second,
a glance of an eye can turn
affection's day-by-day to love.

Grace is less than an instant.
On the spur of a day's moment
we wait. On this alone

Hinges our statement of progress;
balanced between profit and loss,
an accountant's right hand raised.

Journal

Daybreak:
Up with the morning star. On her heels
a rumour of sallow light now spreads
over our horizon. A master hands down
the theme: the sun's trip westwards,
topic for our song, plot for a psalm.

A blind of unconcern night had drawn
over the mind now lifts. Gradually,
we prepare for another journey.
Truth or fable, feast or abstinence,
how is the journal chequered today?

Day's End:
Today the tiniest pretext was enough
to slip away: a telephone's ring,
a letter to answer, a coffee cup,
hubbub, so many matters to attend,
any distraction to evade ourselves,
anything but the price of unbusyness.

Night is falling. We're called once
again to our aloneness. We wonder
which merits most bustle or repose,
fuss and action or a cloister's rigours?
A heaven's desolate star lights up.
To both their due, hermit and hustler.

Psalm in the Night

What kind of turmoil has come
between me and my night's sleep?
Such foolishness! Wake up!

Damn and double damn him,
the funk, the lousy turncoat,
skulking from all I stand for.

But what's the point of my anger,
this belligerent chatter that didn't
snuff the hanger-on, there and then.

Why did I let him away with it?
That swindler. Now alone I examine
twists of my conscience's loudmouth.

Was it lack of spunk, what-it-takes,
or my own too courteous backbone
that made me bend for that louse?

Which was better? To back off
or view the world with his eye?
Lie with a dog, rise with a flea.

A night's trouble throws me between
secrets of two testaments: the old,
the new? But look! already a sun

in darling humour is opening a rift
in my tomb of dark. Mover of light
lure my eye to where well-being lies.

The Patient

It is we whispered,
lightening the unlightenment,
it is the crab!

He's past the paltry skill
of vein and muddy reason
we name the mind.

Fathoming the unsaid,
we scan terror in his eye.
Do you think he knows?

Knows amidst the bevies
of nurses with light laughter
gay and white as linen?

Knows these guarding angels
are no paradise messengers
but gate-keepers of Gethsemane?

Knows hearts moved to pity
harden before cock-crow –
Gethsemane is a lonely garden?

One summer will melt
Memories of winter dark;
Our sorrow drowns in luck

As pain must thaw to joy.
Brave in the jaws of terror,
We worship the overall.

An East Wind
(for prisoners of conscience)

The wind's blowing its scruple,
a long pleading of oppression
eddying from gable to gable
around this Maytime Dublin.
Like rounded fists of confetti
blossoms cluster on cherry trees,
handfuls of memories to scatter.
What does the wind's voice say?

Did you hear the policeman's tap?
They knocked nearby last night.
Did you feel Siberia's frost
Turning bitter, a heart tightening?
Scared, I still stood my ground;
my fears were stitched with trust
until terror froze in my mind,
even my cry for pity dries up.

I hear it whispered in my ear.
Does anyone heed the wind's rustle?
A daily round, a circle of friends
through a train's window veer
and steal away. No returning.
Believe, in the teeth of the wind,
it's for you, my friend, I whistle.

Pacifist

Rebellion's flag hoisted,
my heart-beats flooded
and the crowds tramp by.

Hearing the drum-thump,
my bones remember betrayal,
rekindle in me a pagan.

So, are you hero or whimperer,
soldier or chicken-heart?
Who'd suffer such indignity?

I hear the drummed question.
My pulse loves its answer;
my mind is checking my foot.

Grappling an enemy, I'd see
everything through his eye,
desire only his world.

Empires are seeds in the snow,
Roman, Turkish, Saxon,
every reign an eel's back.

Though no lover of wrongs,
my soul frosts with fear.
Let the drummer pass by.

Three Charms

1. *Against Jealousy*

Even if aggression whets the knife,
a calm mastery has a keener edge.
Consume me in searching out the golden apple
but don't urge the prick of jealousy,
tame in me that wildest beast.

2. *Against Loneliness*

Though I relish action,
on purpose I've chosen a quarantine
to try to reach the core of things.
Don't let it be a friendless renown,
a bait on the hook of loneliness.

3. *Against Despair*

Yesterday's gladness tore me
asunder. Today I pay the reckoning.
The grapnel of despair won't catch me.
I refuse a smooth answer of self-misery.
Well, maybe. Another SOS from MO'S.

Ingebjörg

Just imagine not knowing
the likes of you existed –
but here you spring on us,
a beautiful plump child.
Still a sovereign mistress
careless of place or time –
I name and bless you roly-poly.
Are you my lovely Ingebjörg!

In your eyes I gaze a crystal,
the same once seen in mine,
what lands will you travel –
how often fall in love?
Ingebjörg I speak with you
a language you won't understand,
with only this to tell you:
your mother was a gentle friend.

Ghetto

My ardour is no longer enough.
A prophet in a land with no heir,
a left-behind without a faithful.

If full could understand lean...
Weight of numbers menaces our want,
every thought a surrounding threat.

I plead guilty. Slyly I scheme
to throw off rags of drought,
tatters and patches of famine.

I stand accused. So charge,
not with arrogance or ambition,
just a refusal to die in a cavern.

Leaving is treason for the zealous,
a trespass for the powerful; I understand
Paul, neither Jew nor Gentile.

Yet he didn't shrink. Farewell
to dark. I'm coming to grips
with a world. I hunger for life.

FROM **SPRINGNIGHT**

(1983)

Aubade

The sun has outdated darkness, another morning
pacemakes history, man the word-bearer reawakes
and dares to praise. Begging my tongue of fire,

I proclaim a motto theme, naming in ecstasy
mysteries of time. Always I crave the centre –
serenity suffused by passion, endless and complete.

Although I celebrate, I still hear the metronome's
remorseless beat. No rubato here or emancipation;
accomplices in the scheme, each day is our biography.

It's January. Secretly a season turns its rondo.
In the clue of our rhythm flickers an incarnation,
time and timelessness counter-subjects in this fugue.

In a New York Shoe-Shop

Canned blues rhythms hum the background.
Air-conditioned from the swelter, a choosy
clientele vets the canted wall-racks

of new-look summer shoes. Unbargained for,
a handsome inky coloured man catching
the snappy syncopation, jazzes across the floor

to proof-dance a pair of cream loafers.
Beaming, he bobs and foot-taps; pleased
with his purchase, he jives a short magnificat.

A friend from Maryland had once described
seeing in his grandfather's cellar rusted irons
that had fettered a chain-gang of black slaves.

Behind the polyrhythm, the scoops, the sliding
pitches and turns, I hear the long liquid line
of transcended affliction; women with gay

kerchiefs are prayer-hot in the praise-house
or whoop in Alabama's cotton-fields. Life ad libs
with a jug and washboard; sublimity forgives.

In submission to the pulse, this customer lets go,
swings low to the bitter-sweet quadruple
time, unmuzzled, human and magnificent.

A Resignation

Time has it every way. Changeful,
a moment mirrors the ultimate chance
or multiplies an endless monotony.

Apostles lost in ecstasy don't fret
as terms play follow-the-leader,
each year dispatching another student

generation. Unabashed, the missioner persists –
no lack-lustre, no common room chitchat
erodes his dream. A teacher, he senses

in each disciple the dateless epiphany.
The less blessed, ensnared by fluke or default,
endure the trammels of a chalky despair.

Was it a muse or a gene programmed
to non-conform, a dare-devil compulsion
to waver – then plunging, free-fall alone?

The genuine said 'Good luck with whatever.'
Threatened, the would-be quitter mocks:
'Tell us, what will you do for bread?'

No fanfare. Saunter through a cobbled quad,
an arch, a wickergate half-open to the light.
Tug the ripcord. Faith mushrooms overhead.

Springnight

Framed by our window, trunks and branches
of chestnut trees are handbook illustrations
of arteries, veins charcoaled on a frosty sky.

Unnoticed tee-shaped shoots fuzz the outline.
After a winter's wait an increment is sprung
in slow motion, growth catching us unawares.

Night is falling. The foreground darkens.
A trail of mauve clouds along the skyline
tones into the murk. A change of scene.

I gaze. You, my love, are tucked in sleep.
On edge, I begin the loneness of a night;
all eyes and ears I'm keeping this watch.

Starlight throws a window oblong on our wall,
a screen where homing cars project the trees –
slowly, then rushing back in previews of dawn.

The night will never stay. A half-refrain
from the primary reader unreels in my mind
like a mantra. Will a bird come in on cue?.

A distant lemon streak. The trees blush.
In my vigil a world is disclosing its meaning:
wonderful terror, terrifying wonder of waiting.

Setting Out

Nagging again the starter switch,
I hope the battery cells have hoarded
their fill of ergs and amps.

The choke serves a pick-me-up;
giddily, a current jumps the electrode
gap, begets the holy spark

that fires the inspired mixture
of petrol mist. The pedal gingered,
the chassis shudders in resurrection.

A flutter or two before cams and cranks
co-operate. Pivoting on neutral, we modulate
from gear to gear, from mood to mood.

Engines have their moments and memories.
Now the pistons in their four-stroke cycle
pump, excited as knees on a tandem.

Name the brake linings, the oil sump –
it's Saturday, father in a greasy gaberdine
is sprawled in state, busy under the body.

Mention the spell of a butterfly throttle –
the future opens. A man lives figuratively.
Internally combusting, I lever into overdrive.

Streetscene

The aim fidelity, a perfect wide-angled focus.
But the frames slide into a movie, reality
blurring under a metaphysical Midas touch.
Is this the perpetual street? Spring says yes

as sporting a soft indigo cambray blouse,
a cinnamon suede skirt, a plum-coloured
underskirt jutting below, a young office girl
passes on some mid-morning postal mission.

A lorry driver's mate winks, wolf-whistles
an easy-going admiration; then stoops to lower
through an opened pavement grill another
squat beer cylinder, trundling to the underworld.

Hell must be dumb, a terrible dank cellar
of wonder bottled up, shuttered from the sun,
tight-lipped, tongue-tied, the word slips memory.
Unexposed to worship, we wither in darkroom silence.

Blinking in the sun, this viewfinder rescans
the non-stop synergy of a street. A child chases
a coin pirouetting over a gutter; touching each other
two greying men swap hush-hush information.

A flower-seller highlights, proclaims her titles:
freesia, tulip, anemone. A whitsun gift.
Crouched, the sound-man records the sacred words,
open-sesames unlock again the gate of Babel's Tower.

Early Irish Lyric

Once again picture him near St Gall,
a monk in exile. Cinctured, diligent,
he is glossing, paving a Latin grammar.

'There are persons in the noun and particle,
though they are infinite!' He annotates a text
with his cryptic memory aids. Today's

lesson prepared, he unbends, daydreams.
It is early morning. Suddenly fired,
high on the elixir of spring, he declares:

'A hedge of trees overlooks me; for me
a blackbird sings – news I won't conceal...'
Febrile, meticulous, he chronicled the astoundment

a thousand years ago on the lower edge
of a vellum folio. This is another spring
and we are brothers conjugate in ecstasy.

Something ignites. Possessed by the flame
the psyche hums. On a jag of ink
a nib travels in *delirium tremens.*

Fashion Show

Out in the daylight green is the rage,
chlorophyll the mode. Trees let it all
hang out while indoors poor leafless
sophisticates of shape and dye present
a spring collection. Quietly sensational
in magenta, lilac, beige or stone,
high stepping ladies arm for summer.

Models turn our heads with ready-made
come-hither smiles, lope in a spotlight's
circle, splash their favours of layering
and fabric, whisk past in giddy colours;
a final bout, then swishing down the steps,
unbuttoning, they breakneck for a cubicle.
We await another creation. Meantime

three new mannequins swirl on stage,
ambush the eye: the compère patters on:
'Now a summer dress in china blue
with scalloped hem.' How can they dream
up such stratagems, the tuck and cut
to self-assure, frazzle the male to ask
no whys or wherefores. O lovely woman!

No! Stop! The tease will unman me –
if only they'd speak, say something
unreasonable to slow desire, but those
body linguists show no leniency,
beaming all the more they swoop
across the platform. Bewitched again,
fall a little for these frame-dames!

Easter

Dizzy with joy, the Easter morning
sun trembles in the heavens;
the tacky buds unclenched, release
an appropriate festschrift of leaves.

Unsuspected, in their microworld
tiny cells teem, crossplay,
rich networks of twisted strings
interlace, relate to the concord

of history rebegun. A starling mimics
Bravura, wood-pigeons whoop it up,
the orchestra purrs, tunes into
a master craftsman. Life *da capo*,

as riding our whirling earth-ship
we zip around the sun;
umpteen billion miles apart
stars both giant and dwarf

are suns that tug their planets,
constellate, take their partners
to dance the zillionhanded reel,
pinwheel outwards to eternity.

Glimpsing infinities of perfection,
awestruck, half-enlightened man
refracts the marvel, magnifies
an all-inclusive Easter thought.

Dún Laoghaire Pier

Shivering, I often stood on deck to watch these arms
greeting us as the ferry slid between the cutstone
fists on into the bosom. But lazing on a Mayday noon,
suntrapped in the elbow of the west pier, I luxuriate

in its enormous repose. Occasional joggers lumber past,
a lady calls a wayward dog; the wind jingles shrouds
of a moored yacht, a blue-jibbed dinghy dawdles by.

Make-believe. Slip a century back, daydream a fleet
of brown-sailed trawlers, coal-boats with grimy deckhands
like minstrels blacked for a show. Clean-stone lighthouses
on the pier-ends are thumbs up to passing merchant ships,
cruisers, frigates. Grey-coated, red-cuffed constables
with glazed hats patrol busy quays. Sea-captains intrigue
in power-houses, tussle for the berth of harbour master.

The pier-wall, a crazy pavement of granite and sandstone
glistens: now along its base dandelions clump in garlands
for those unnamed, who slaved with caissons, shunted
wagonloads of boulders. The fittest survived outbreaks
of cholera, riots, strikes; a thousand plus they reckon
squatted on Dalkey common, bullied rocks from the quarry.
In their embrace I consecrate a morning to their memory.

Wounds

Who wasn't wounded on the way, doesn't ferry
Scattered in the flesh shrapnel memories of a failure,
Grapple with fears that, fed on, a fragment buried
In the self, could sour the blood, infect the brain?
You planned the scalpel's cool careful incision;
Then, cutting briskly through the scarskin excised
Dead tissue of those old sores. That eagle vision,
Lady-hand and lion-heart. A pain is exorcised.
Transplanted thoughts restore the damaged cells;
Skin-grafting pocks and scars you face-lift sorrow,
Implant the mind with germs of bliss. A presence
Tones my morning, each evening fulfils a promise.
Nursed by affection, slowly I choose to grow;
Removing lesions, your love is surgeon to the soul.

Post-Operative

Green-blue medicos in bakers' hats
mazed about the ante-theatre –
friends, my fear was measureless!

Limp, by ward sisters rewoken,
shaken back from semi-dead,
grateful, I welcome reincarnation.

Lazarus, this is wonderful! Though
tell me did you, like me, look back
on faithless moments before the dark;

feel forgiveness lagged with linen,
touch this sheet or hear in hints
far-off laughter guest a neighbour?

A shade surreal beyond a towel,
flimsily glance flowers and grapes,
taste another sensational chance?

Body-weak but glad to be
heed anew the hand of joy.
Can even this still-life laud?

Birch

When winter darkens the urge
I've wavered. Losing my verve,
I doubt even a nudging mover.
What is it nerves again the sap?

Discreetly, buds bring out a year's
débutantes. Curious as mouse-ears,
vivacious, petite, see-through
leaves spring into the life-light.

Barely condoning such frivolity,
a stoic, this narrow white tree
indulges its limbs, though its trunk
wears a black belt all through summer

in spoil-sport memory of a fall.
The ascetic birch now waits
for autumn's curtain call to remove
its make-up, throw off the frippery.

Another year curves to completion,
signing a circle deep in the stock;
reason is cyclical – while upwards
love swerves seasons in a spiral.

Lady at Cocktail Party

Somewhere in a middle distance
I'm your admirer. The overall
tonal key, the emotive texture
evolves around your presence;
my childlike perspective conceptual,
every movement aspires,
all lines and curves allude
to you; honeypot of attention,
epicentre of our foreground.

Woozy, a little out of sync,
stills reel, the movie takes,
a whole assemblage of images,
successive changes of form
reposition, pass by, leave
elusive impressions on the eye;
walk-on parts are bleared
second-bests, extras unfocused
by you, the leading lady.

Freeze again the party scene
so I can revel in one frame
with you my lovely centre-piece
in black stilettos and stockings,
a blouse and low-crowned
hat to match with red
ribbons reflecting a mid-calf
culotte; a thoughtful
study in red and black.

After-Image

Curious, rubber-necking through landing banisters,
we sneaked glimpses, in suspense waited or snooped
by the drawing-room door to overhear a mumble
of conclave as mother detailed the portfolio:
the bedroom would be off the scullery; duties
entailed the daily haul of our home affairs.

Night out Tuesday, half-day Thursday and Sunday.
Those strange times when girls from the country
in a pinafore uniform kept halfway house,
chored for their board. The fortunate, dancing
on their evening out or the August holiday find
a husband, bow themselves out. Children,

all nuances blunted, we borrow an older sister.
Mary, Molly, Kathleen – the names return
even if the faces smudge a little, trick
recollection. Incredible how lives once woven
inexorably slip and drift. Still they survive

Distant figures in the fretwork of the memory,
scatter-hoarded after-images of our affection.

Schoolboy Final

At each corner flag-sellers double-deal.
Colour-parties of schoolboys stump, file
through turnstiles, bustle to the stands.

A hub-bub swells while banners, mascots
swirl and vie: already togged cheer-leaders
megaphone their slogans. One commissar

glancing towards the field, eyes someone's
sister among the schoolgirl camp-followers;
concentration wavers, resumes as a battle-cry.

Huddled between factions, inwardly fluttering
parents affect a sangfroid: 'let's hope they're
evenly matched.' A warrior-priest chain-smokes.

Furore. Two squads erupt into the arena,
flexing, limbering. A pent-up frenzy
steadies, runs up, kicks. Life in parenthesis.

The sun raids the pitch, angling spring-light
past a grandstand gable; the crowd's chant
surges and slumps as chance twirls the volume.

Loose ruck, the ball tunnelled back, picked
up, a long looping pass, well-gathered, chipped
forward. On the attack. Commenting in the lingo

the old-timers' adrenalin empathises; reruns,
inklings of cosmos within cosmos reconnoitre
life as an enthusiasm. The world turns seventeen.

Father

After Sunday lunch, gentle with wine and garlic
snuggled in a fug of cigarsmoke, he nods, drops
into ritual doze. Anxious about draughts, tiptoeing,
gingerly protective, we spread a rug on his lap.

That sleep-mask fascinates. His features belie his age
though the hair is now wisps. 'I declare to God,'
he reported lately, fingering the crown of his head,
'given another year, I'll be as bald as a coot.'

Asleep, a frame so fragile denies a presence
encompassing my childhood until the push and pull
of growth unravelled its cocoon. Secret recollections
sneak across the room, savouring moods of afternoon.

Awake again. Sharpening a congenital zest for language,
craftsmen, we tackle the deadly serious business
of a crossword. Synonyms, cognates pun, criss-cross
in double-meanings. Nonplussed I turn apprentice.

In the evening a ceremonial drink, then music.
Pleading age, he recoils from the wistful; so Strauss's
Perpetual Motion spins on the turntable as father
reminisces, summons mythologies of memory; a favourite

the night he danced the *Lambeth Walk* in Casablanca.
Listening, I reflect on our comradeship. It isn't
who follows or fathers whom; infinitely more subtle,
our courses parallel, plot to converge on a horizon.

For a Child

Strange, how I feel I've a stake in you,
starting another lap. A few years his senior
I was commandeered by neighbours to chaperon
their son to school. That son is your father.

No blood relation, my intentions only spiritual,
but in reckoning your career, you'll forgive
one secular question: is speed inherited?
Your father was an athlete, sprinter and wing.

I wonder what masterplan chromosomes submit
what information unloads, messages transmit,
self-replicating, relaying a human marathon;
eons of genes culminate, uncode in you.

Such possibilities converge! Yet you take
the fuss in your stride. Already I have seen
you flash your mother's smile; catching
the gist of living, you stow your memories.

Someway I think you know we're fêting
your entry to the race. Reassured, quickened
by your incarnation, the absurd recedes.
A baton passed, our thoughts turn forward.

Homeward

After climbing, we level out. Tuned to a ground-station
our yaw self-adjusts while trusting to the whirl
and pitch of turbo-props, we move by inspiration.

Streamlined, believing in magnetic flux, we navigate.
Over these months, I have indulged freedoms of a man
in love to admire the beauty of every woman I met.

Yet mindful of Icarus, I'm glad each pivoted needle
in the cockpit's angled maze of switch and dial
swings homeward. All thoughts now focus on you.

It has been a long continence. Love knows
feast and fast. Parted only by an hour
I dream, unfasten a little long-distance libido.

The first frenzy of unison over, we'll bask
in a routine, relearning the daily shuttle
of union and separation, love's drag and thrust.

So the approach. Our undercarriage untucked,
flaps curved, windward we surge then sink;
closed throttle, nose up, we touch down.

Late Beethoven Quartet

Proud brainowner, once a Napoleon fan,
he pounded heaven's door. Those drum rolls
now acquiesce in a throb of equanimity.

Quadruple beauty: a risqué violin trend-sets
the cello's ruminant assent; prudent fiddle,
work-a-day viola interject a casual symmetry.

Motifs then fragment, configurations interweave,
mix, shapeshift with maniacal precision –
a reckless accelerando of distilled simplicity.

A poise not a posture; no truculent stance
toys here with despair. The word is praise,
the theme a scale of infinite permutation.

Elegy for a Singer

Fevered woman too quick afire,
song-queen too giving glowed
over, fuelled a chiller world.

Heady days ago we played
love together; two limelighters
moodchanged, flamed and quenched.

That was then not now; so why
self-condemn, regret delight –
No how nineteen years could fathom

slower growths of fondness; but
know that always after parting
I cherished you. Now, girl, goodbye!

Mastermind demands you leave,
quit the dance in swing and drive,
lonely take the last route home.

Still a little my once sweetheart,
rest a while and then farewell;
travel gently the forever zone.

Seepage

Eight painstaking years we'd strained to cheat
Mistrust, to fill this sea, to take the plunge –
Swim in each other's confidence; with one deceit
The ocean floor is porous, bedrock again a sponge.
Who'd have thought the sea could leak? Naïve,
We took no soundings, dismissed all our fears,
But shallowing us, you siphoned our will to believe
And sieved away the sum of both our years.
So I'm your fall-guy, high and dry. Yet younger
By half, I watch you growing frailer, thinner faced.
Afraid that time may ache with retrospective hunger,
I covet this chance. We've no time to waste!
Beginning the slow penance of a seeped devotion,
We spoon-feed trust, thimble back the ocean.

Thank-You Note

Thank you for walking at Enniskerry. Rhododendrons,
a copper stream supplied the mobile backdrop
for our wonderland of thought. Those currents
of talk and silence seem to gather and pattern
the logic of a year's biography. Splicing experience,
we catch the astonishment in a sunburst of laughter.

Friendships know no genealogy, yet carefully grafted
knit like bones strengthened, braced by the mend.
Still we behave oddly. For four leap years
we've seldom met to layer our common ground;
content with heartwood, annual rings surround us
in brotherhood. Is time only of the essence?

Implicated in each other's story, the sap is mutual.
Long after meetings, hints, strange underplots,
asides, hunches in an interrogative mood re-emerge
as subterfuges of growth, burgeon by remote control.
Alone I chuckle. Infinity is the root of friendship.
Amazed remembrance explodes in an endless thank-you.

April Soliloquy

Give just an omen, the merest sign
the word is not ill-spent. But a subtle
all-wise unfolds the birch's larva bud
a token to endorse a winter of thought.

Along Dublin's suburban roads, cherry
trees market their blossoms, the late
April breezes are throwing fistfuls
of confetti to sway and freak and fall.

Syllables of a soliloquy, planned obsolescence.
Something overspills, flows in a eulogy.
Part of this nature, I accumulate in delight
a sinking fund against a reckoning day.

Gainful as a hermit's centripetal thought
or a pick-up needle skating the grooves
to a great finale, spellbound in perfect
concentration, everything is new to say.

A plectrum plucks the nerve of joy.
Nothing but the word contains the intensity.
A profusion. Sudden headiness of being.
Is life itself the burning bush?

FROM **THE IMAGE WHEEL**

(1985)

Invocation

The nerve-threads are strings
on a violin, out of the heart
winds the ribbon of melody.

Round and round the potter's lathe,
life lurches in a spinning wheel,
the giddy ghost of the trinity.

Let me dance, let me dance,
give me the madness for the waltz,
three great beats of eternity.

Morning on Grafton Street

Grafton Street is yawning, waking
limb by limb; jewellers' steel
shutters clatter upwards, the sweet
doughy smells from hot-bread

shops steam the frosty morning,
warm our passing; disc-stores'
sudden rhythms blare an introit,
launch the busy liturgy of day.

Look! Two breakfast wooers
fallen in love with farewells
smooch, soul-kiss on the kerb.
Gently, my street puts on her face.

Grafton Street, witness of my time,
seer, watcher of every mood,
traps me the grandeur, the melancholy,
ever-new carnival of man.

Walk here alone in broodiness,
inwoven, anonymous, swept along;
stroll here infatuated, self-communing,
lost in the lyric flow of street.

Lunchtime in a London Café

Table by table the café fills
till talk and the clap of plates
bulge with well-being; a dark
waitress's patchwork skirt
hurries behind the counter;
every face under the sun peers
at the window menu, more
voices join the steamy pentecost.

Here in the metropolis nothing
shocks. Out of its huge anonymity
worlds of strange gossip crowd
this lunch-time café. And I'm in love
with its mystery, the peculiar rapture
of life à la carte. The window mists;
after wine, the Basque in the corner
turns his smokey eyes on the waitress.

Outside the door, the buses shriek,
rush and judder; a city's jamboree,
hope and haphazard, limitless
chances, choices wait. Sitting
here I know I've felt the throb
of Jerusalem or Rome or any city
yet to come, where there's a café
and we, citizens all, break bread.

Ode to a Juggler

Such style! The incredible untroubled
Faraway look of twice-doubled
Concentration: one, two, three, four.

One ball caught by the crook of the neck,
She steadies a little to countercheck
The rhythm, tosses it back into orbit.

Five. There's a long career ahead;
A genius called Rastelli once fed
The air with ten at a time. But there

Among the primroses, in on the grass,
This juggler entertains us as we pass
On more urgent business. Short-cutting

Through the park most must adhere
To the narrow path of errand; for a mere
Moment we stop to watch, wonder if

Her playfulness mocks our humdrum worth.
The balls roll in mesmeric mirth,
jokes told with flawless timing,

Or are they stars held in motion,
Not by gravity but by devotion
To a great god of fun? Seemingly

Unaware of our admiration, she enthralls.
The endless edgeless tennis balls
Move in the abandon of her serenity.

Fly-By

Bone-weary, my nerves played out,
nothing in the mind turns over, takes off.

Seated by the window I'm gaping,
praying for a happening to lift the soul.

Out of the blue, a coal-tit has splashed
down on the wet balcony railing.

His head twitters, his eye uneasy
follows a magpie who is hedge-hopping

menacingly below. Darting downwards
his spindle legs cling to a bar

like climbing irons. Still he jerks,
carries out this probe manoeuvre

then drops, docks in the flower-box.
Gobbling a crumb his throat pouch

bulges and shrinks; a sudden invisible
signal from mission control orders

a dash to the edge, a quick check
before the lift-off. Refreshed, I'm

happy to broadcast the commentary,
privileged to be a flight-recorder.

Fathers and Sons

Time's an old man lifting his glass,
toasting life and saying, 'Son,

no one can sound another's depth,
alone, alone fathom the well-shaft –

the long clanging fall from the sun,
the draught upwards back to light.'

Time's a young man's swaying bucket
slapping water over its brink.

Letters from Assisi

1. *Francis to his Father*

Father, if only you'd understood
I craved to be the man of every hour –
All your ambition slept deep in my blood.

I loved the touch of silk, the feel of power,
To gossip, joke, outshine Assisi's cavaliers;
For all that talk of bird or flower

I'd your merchant's will to vie. Two years
Caught a prisoner in Perugia, I was still
Half-aware I'd fought for a town's profiteers.

A ransom. Then, the homecoming. 'Is Francis ill
Or in love?' people asked, wondered why
I looked so distant. I did the parties until

Something snapped. Every stricken passer-by
Now fixed his stare on me, saying 'Francis,
All turns on you; Francis, look me in the eye!'

There were riches in Apulia; I'd lances,
Troubadours' songs to sing. I could forget.
But haunted daily by those strangers' glances,

I sold your bale of cloth to let
Some paupers eat. Father, you whipped me,
Branded me a madman; each time we met

You cursed me, so I paid a down-and-out a fee
To bless me as his father, taunt your sorrow –
I wanted to outdo, best the world in poverty.

I was so young and life was tomorrow.
Already my followers scheme for a benefice.
The road seemed short – I could beg or borrow

Rags of humility, call your care avarice.
Time unlocks compassion's garden-gate.
Father, can you forgive my Judas kiss?

2. *Francis to Clare*

My Clare, in years to come they'll
puzzle over us! *Francesco e Chiara.*
I can almost hear them chuckle.
Let them wonder! If they don't know
that love's first sight can seal
a lifetime, how will they understand?
You came to me when I already
was sworn to Mistress Poverty.
Saints carry their souls in lovely
vessels, only iron wills have made
our rule. There's a thousand ways

to know another; we may not share
the daily buzz and flittings of a mind.
Each alone in prayer acclaims this love,
still in the cell of its first perfection.

3. *Francis to his Followers*

You know the joy and stigma we the prophets wear?
Bat just an eyelid and the splinter newness of another
Reborn wisdom dims. Only a while, my brothers!
Although I didn't see each knot in the net of time,

As any visionary tiptoeing the fringes of his sanity
I glimpsed an image-god hiding in the mind of man;
As every mender of history takes up his strand,
I tied a love-knot, hitched my thread to the work.

Magellan

How could I know if I dreamt or raved?
Night after night in Oporto's taverns
I ran my finger around a globe
of wine, caressing the lure of a curve.

Loud in the torchlight beggared veterans
talked of gold; my thoughts drifted west,
below the Line, then through a strait,
probing a thread of South Sea islands.

Monsoons blow through the palm leaves,
canoes race over a deep lagoon;
fame is where the orange-tree blossoms.
Shipless mariner, did you dream or rave?

Still I believed it all would happen.
Months of sodden hope against chance,
combing the mutinous reefs and shallows.
Magellan, Magellan, are you mad?

Follow the flagship, ask no questions!
El Paso – I wept when we passed
The Lands of Fire and fled for summer.
Soon the sky had turned to brass.

We drained butts of yellowed water.
The watch changed, the sand-glass ran –
the mind is the most capricious ocean –
Magellan, where's your land of spice?

Memory shrinks those days to one.
A late March morning, over the horizon
a canoe glided; among their gifts
I saw a Chinese jar. All my life

surrenders to the sublety of its sphere.
'Men,' I shout, 'the world is measured –
as these figures painted around a jar
our names etched on the curve of time!'

I never doubted the signs and wonders.
Yet, like Thomas, I needed the wound.
I wrapped my hands around that jar –
Then I knew I dreamt, not raved.

Einstein

Caught in the rhapsody, I watched a pipe's smoke
cloud and twist its thousand shapes of magic;
walking in shallow summer water, at each footfall
a puff of sand mushroomed and I was afraid.

Will a mind stretching to grope an essential statement
find that galaxies have followed the same equation?
Attentive as a man learning a language from his lover,
I heard amazing rules among sweet nothings.

Homage

Nearly eighty, slow-paced,
stooped, he enters. Even his suit
has seen better days; but touching
that instrument, his face is chamois

which puckers, ripples each phrase;
a smile inscrutable, ears pricked
for an inward zing, heard deep
in the calm of age. This virtuoso

Vlado Perlemuter a half-century
ago, Ravel's apprentice, played
these pieces for the maître whom
in his turn Fauré had fostered.

Lineage of love, strange dynasty
beyond the blood, every succession
wills on the gift; a current
skips from fingertip to tip

along life-giving lines, as once,
suddenly, thumbing through a treasury
we find ourselves, stumble on
forerunners who forefather us.

Warmed by homage, a melody resung
reddens again the afterglow;
son to many far-flung fathers,
there are sons who watch for you.

Memoir

Thoughts lain years
untouched stir and so
find courage to recall
her. At last I dare
burgle childhood's archive,

gather up the collage,
knowingly now probe,
search in thanks to word
the marvel of a woman
once this man's globe.

Watch her again,
mistress of her bureau,
thick in wire-filed
dockets, monthly tots,
tallies – there sits
a wasted Kaiserin.
Look deeper. Alone
a silent novelist
unreels in commonplace
another otherworld.

Herself an only child,
hours she spellbound
traced in her father's
line, the tangle-saga
of his dozen siblings –
how Bill ran away,
took the king's shilling,
died young. This
lonely epic still
marches my middle brain.

Prayers down to earth –
beadless fingers tapped
aloud a rhythm litany:
St Anthony, Pius the Tenth,
Blessed Martin de Porres,
protect us from infectious
diseases. Poems mystified;
she laughed: a pity
to keep a man idle,
so little keeps busy.

One winter evening
breathtook, struck
terror when pulling
open the tallboy's

bottom drawer she
uncovered business-like
winding-sheet and candles
once her mother's, next
her own – we children
should know in case.

Black-haired, oily-skinned
crown prince to those
genes, grateful heir
to many-mooded raptures,
quivers in the dance –
in daily brinkmanship
every twitch, gesture
remembers her in me.
All blunted whetted,
what smouldered burns.

A Short Biography

Tell me, friend, how this began.
Was it that morning you tricycled
up the slope along the path
to the woods; wheeling around,
pedalling frantically homewards,
snowflakes spun in the trees,
and passing through the garden gate,
you turned forever into Eden?

Or maybe one winter afternoon,
alone in the sittingroom listening
to music on a radio left idling
after the news, you were staring
through the window, when suddenly
the trance-dance stirred? Then
all was transfigured. Again
you'd blundered into seventh heaven.

Or the autumn evening carrying back
messages from the shop, you watched
a man stooping to bundle the last
sheaves? The yellow stooks ranked
sunwards, the damp seed-smell
of corn seized you; startled,
a half-dazed witness to the majesty,
you climbed over the narrow stile.

A Fall

Late one night we found him in a drunken doze,
curled up on the frozen pavement, his fullmoon
face and stub-nose shining snugly in fuddlement.

We knew him to see; by all accounts a stage genius
bound for the summit – yet somehow he slithered, blew
his chance, bungled, stood great impresarios up.

A mountaineer keen on the climb, the low trail,
the long hike, steady tedious uphill trek,
till sheer handhold over foothold, ledge by ledge

he peaks – then scanning the grandeur of his vista,
senses guilt, misses the hazard of ascent; dizzy,
feeling the odds creep up against him, he slips.

We dragged him to his feet. Gathering a rugged dignity
he managed *comrades!* – mounted the steps to his door.
Anxious below, we watched the windows for light.

Meeting

We both chose to sphere another world,
To wheel and turn around a different sun,
So since when circles touched or curled
In tandem, meetings seemed a duty done.
An eye which flicks a mock surprise, a stab

Of doubt now mars your words, reveals a new
Control, a silted fear that I might blab –
In shedding former secrets unorbit you.
Our fields unlike, we spin on separate poles
But still are fuelled on memories shared by both;
Each fed on gravity, pulled by different goals –
Must we disown our commonwealth of growth?
I owe you too much to push such memories aside,
At every tangent, I long for our suns to coincide.

For My Friends

Spendthrift friendships once ravelled and unravelled,
Carefree leisurely as a journey without a plan;
Easy-come, easy-go, there was a while I travelled
Lightly, made my friends catch-as-catch-can.
Gradually, the casual twisted the precious weave,
This tissue of feeling in which I have grown;
Though I follow a single thread, I must believe
That bound to the whole we never drift alone.
Crossed, matted fibres long inwrought,
Friendships prove the fabric of a common story,
The web which takes the strain of every thought,
Shares the fray or stain, joys in our glory.
Interwoven, at last I dare to move without misgiving;
I touch the invisible, love this gauze of living.

Listening

Afraid for you, hastily I interfere,
Advising this or that to avert
Another danger and so appear

To chart your course. Salt in a hurt –
Though I would be Job's Elihu –
My words sting. In pain you blurt:

'Friends pick my sores, outdo
Each other in choosing the wisest plan
To mend my ways. Now it's you.

Easy for you, you chanty man,
To know the ropes by rhythm and song!
Words of wisdom scorn me. How can

You fathom my affliction? I belong
To those troubled who must grieve
Alone. The weak are a riddle for the strong.'

Humbly I concur; but the heart, naïve
In its listening, begs you to hear
The silent rhythm's call and heave.

Scruples

> *or the day's vanity, the night's remorse*
> – YEATS

Comrade, pilot of my travels,
You have given generous light –
Yet an inner voice cavils;

Prophet–poet by what right?
Self-doubt and scruples hover,
Conscience cries by night.

How can I now recover,
Redeem your years spent
Loving the bemused half-lover?

Double-mated, I never meant
To fail, to shortfall you;
The moodchanger muse has leant

On me, squeezed more than due;
Untrue, undertakings broken,
I forfeit my claims on you.

Excuses too smooth-spoken,
Words shallow at source –
Comforts too soft to token

Divided pain or to endorse
My shame, that counter-theme
Matching your sorrow with remorse.

Can nothing I do or dream
Charge a cell of resurrection
Bring again love on stream?

Amazed at such introspection,
'Love,' you whisper, 'why remorse,
am I not queen of my affection?'

Blues

When demons dance, even you must
Dare again the threat of dust;
Those days you too will falter.
Undone by rifts of self-distrust

You mope, try once more to persuade
Yourself, saying 'If only I'd made
Other choices; where now are all
My might-have-beens? I'm afraid.

I'm straying, losing my clue to the maze.
Surely I could find other ways
To serve?' No, it must be so!
Although you turn back to praise,

Only fools won't hear this rumble
Between the panegyric lines. A humble
Song manoeuvres in the hinterland
Of hope. You too must stumble.

Pardon yourself. Then feel the shove
Onward, a booster, until above
And beyond the image-wheel turns,
Spins from doubt fables of love.

Somewhere

A cluster of girls, busy
with gossip, are laughing,
hearing what's new, they
whisper names, dropping
hints of a timeless land.

Deft in their sleep
lovers turn in the night,
nudge back together,
sovereign in this kingdom,
no-man's-land of trust.

Suddenly, waking in the strange
borderland of darkness,
a child is crying. The mother-
hand relights the lamp,
kindles the hum of sleep.

Slack in an October sun
the calm of old stagers
again seems to say:
time is no fastland,
measure only by light.

Somewhere in the outlands
a man listens. All history
fidgets in this heart, aching
to uncode a word
hidden in the moment's pathos.

Rebels

So once you wished to clean-sweep the world –
first outfling of hurt, fledgling's overreach.
In fuller flight we wheel an earth-shaking circle
of loyal friends, throw light or shadow,
soar or sweep, rebels within that sacred theatre.

Weather the knowing nod, the foolproof remark:
'So at last he's seen the light.' As if a youth-
long hope could pass blighted by a moment, bubble
blown, pebble skimmed over water. Believe me, brother,
mellowed we serve, lifetime comrades of a dream

harmony where each anguish shared soon resolves,
passing dissonance, spice-notes in sweeter melodies
of being. Gentler, we fly closer to the wind,
let life slip through logic's web until we glance
a scheme in the million-coloured spectrum of our praise.

Absence

On my own I swore I'd settle calmly down:
Hours later, plans threadbare, my mind hovers
Uneasily; again I wander the evening town,
My aloneness grazed by each pair of passing lovers.
Halved, my life is now unreal, as though,
Rootless, the everyday events are tossed
Around in uncompleted reverie; in midflow
You left a sentence, the conversation's theme is lost.
We too have myths, symbols, a world of our own,
A universe of tangled memories, hopes and schemes;
Counterpoised within that dovetailed zone,
We share our chosen take-for-granted dreams.
Without you, my love, too many thoughts unspoken,
Words are babble, a sacred thread is broken.

Loss

The last summer he walked slower, chose to linger.
Pausing in a laneway, he ran a thumb along the seam
of an old garden wall – 'Those joints need pointing'
he warned; attentive, we saw in his face some strange
play of inward movement. On request we drove to Meath;

those fields a dozen times the size of his own
pleasured his eye. At Christmas leaning on the window sill,
Lovingly, he gazed over a few loamy acres towards Gola.
In mid-January, cutting back briars, he fell with his scythe.

Several years later, I waken deep into the night,
hear you sobbing to yourself. It's Patrick's Eve,
That evening your father used return after
his winter exile, a labourer in Scotland; three
eager children watch the dark beyond Dunlewy.
Now, at last, the bus's headlamps arc the sky –
overjoyed you race the lights to meet him at Bunbeg.
Tonight, here by your side I listen, then kissing
your forehead, throw my arms around your sorrow.

Nocturne

Life burns low. Lounging,
relishing the movement and repose,
balanced ease of late evening,
lazy eyes free-lance. There,
orbed in lamplight you browse.

Occasional comments log a day.
No statement, merely venerate
detail: bright red plant-pot,
blue-pattern covered cushions,
softly lit in your sphere.

Thriving in the outglow of the hour,
calm globe of wellbeing,
we bed the seed, incubate
thoughts, warm tomorrow's theme.
Hazy, ready to grow in sleep,

sorrow's long shadows fall
beyond the nimbus of our lamp.
We huddle in the kernel. Cares
drown outside love's circle,
blurs well-flooded out by light.

Notes in the mind treasure up
this moment's tune; a melody
finds words to wrap the night,
hoard a measureless memory,
gather our instant into eternity.

Autumn Report

Nel mezzo del cammin di nostra vita
        – DANTE ALIGHIERI

Autumn is touching us with a summer's afterthought.
The tilted sun hazes around the yellow-fringed
branches of maples, eking out our tapered season.
Soon an occasional dash of tangerine will singe
these leaves as even now a few frizzled casualties
butterfly in the hint of a breeze; September, a chancy
friend, blows hot and cold, yet caution cramps us in –
fritters the grand event – so propped in this sidestreet
doorway, a gap on the pavement between two vans
affords a patio where sunlight swabs our regrets,
loosens the mind to osmose the indelible past,
balance its books. Let this sun-captured moment be
a throw-away line, a fly-leaf dedication that stretches
to reach the essence, snatch the tenor of the whole.

Hardheaded Vikings used to figure their age by winters,
but further south, we may chance a count in summers.
I've lived a round three dozen – one over the half
of man's allotment; moving into the second moiety
I tender friends and shareholders an interim report:

Even in this fall, wholehearted life reverberates
some almighty gaiety, invites me to adore
the immense integrity; wines my veins until
I'm sure my frame will warp under such
exuberance. I've never felt so near the centre
of all that is.

        There goes another rumpled
leaf, frisking and nose-diving in the draught

as if to ask what has the whippersnapper new
to say? Today's sun has never shone before,
never found me in this doorway; history has
accumulated this moment, now funnels through me
the urge to utter. In this instant I'm Adam
the first to mouth, to feel the garden overflow
in word and rhythm.

Yes, there were certain liabilities
to meet: mornings which would not wake, days
that moped and brooded on their failure until
shame, an unfed stomach, turned the acid fuel
to gnaw the lining. Dozing on, I recapped each collapse,
idly watched the digital clock matchstick
away my time, slip noiselessly into desperation.
Yet reaffirmed by woman's ardour, again allowed
untense, surrender afresh to laughter, I have
unjailed the self. Some all-embracing love
forgives my shortfall and I am glad to present
this reconciled account.

But a statement is current,
the entrepreneurial everyday rushes forward
to speculate all over again and we who traffic
in life must venture on. Why hedge our bets
or play too cool; detached we might miss
the passion to broaden the bore, deepen the joy?

The wind freshens, risks another leaf or two,
floats some unbidden debenture. Please give me
a few moments more, just to exult in this
last reflux of summer, luxuriate in its praise.
Then gambling on, I'll bless the breeze and go.

THE CHOSEN GARDEN

(1990)

I. DEPARTURE

Baciami sulla bocca, ultima estate.
Dimmi che non andrai tanto lontano.
Retorna con l'amore sulle spalle,
ed il tuo peso non sarà più vano.

Kiss me on the mouth, final summer
Tell me you will not go far away.
Come back with love on your shoulders,
and your weight will no longer be in vain.

> SANDRO PENNA
> (trs. Alessandro Gentili
> & Catherine O'Brien)

Espousal

Days early, my trousseau lay in the hallway,
Mother's own school trunk newly hinged,
freighted as prescribed – all regalia
taped and numbered: rug, napkin ring,
tuck-box, laundry bags. Hour by hour
a dreamy September holds its breath.

Late evening, a scuffle of gravel as cars
brake on the castle's forecourt. Novices
reconnoitre, bustle of arrivals, goodbyes,
last advices, and already I fidget, eager
to embrace my venture; parting promises:
a visit in a fortnight; waves in the half-light.

Down the marble steps into the vast
corridor of wainscotting and notice boards,
lists of placings for study-hall and chapel;
chance meetings, the territory explored –
playrooms, libraries. The tug of a bell,
a hush and we file towards night-prayers.

So, this is the honeymoon of my fantasy,
a reverie of quads, pillow fights, decent
chaps with parcels and cads in Coventry...
My friend was coming, I begged to be sent.
'You're on your own', father has warned,
'you've made your bed, now lie in it.'

Ten twenty. Lights out in the Holy Angels,
we slide into iron beds; a skittish
silence falls; in earshot another dormitory,
same prayer, commanding flick of switch.
Neighbours whisper introductions: Michael
Walls, Roscommon; Flannery from Tipperary.

Snatches of a parlance, subliminal spells:
all out, lectio brevis, night-squares,
smoke in the mind; days to come
gleam, a jingling clump of mortise keys.
I espouse a new world, drop into sleep;
expectation whirrs in the tongues of bells.

Initiation

By hearsay beginners fear the passage rite:
dark talk of toilet dousing and shamings.
Watch your step. Last year's weaklings lord
a brief revenge – *old scout's preference.*
To endure is everything; so now bide time.
Day by day the hierarchical bluff is called.
Seats at table fixed by scramble, the head
holds sway, portions out the food at whim,
waylaying second helpings for his table-top
cronies. It's Monday. Roly-poly and custard
for dessert; O'Sullivan acts the tough, threatens
to confiscate my share...Outside I tackle him;
a flurry of punches, I fall in a stranglehold.
Days later another flare-up; again he wins.
His taboo endangered, we have settled down
to a sultry peace. Fantasy slips into reality.
Inmates of a world slowly, slowly enamoured

of our narrow purlieus, every rule and loophole,
bounds and out of bounds, little by little
we grow fond of our containment. After dinner
in the hamper-room cutting a slice of cake
One of *the hards* comes wheedling, menacing
give us a scrounge! Swear at him loudly –
grinning, he moves on. The weeks pass,
the fittest thrive. No Joyce, no Stephen Dedalus,
your ghost may sulk on the Third Line crease,
baulk at our scramble, but your gaze is hindsight.
We think we dream of home and all the while
who got *sleeps* or a parcel, who made the team,
shifts of comradeship, rumours of a prefect's mood,
concerns, subterfuges map our hours and fill
an atlas of our living. We're in love with survival.
All other worlds are slipping out of reach.

Icons

I stir an entourage of ghosts, icons of youth.
On Sunday nights by turns a sermon. Curious
in the pews, watch the red pine sacristy doors.
Enter tonight's turn, stoled and surpliced,
a gladiator in this fastidious arena: Reverend
J. Burden, S.J., Father Procurator, head high,
manner aloof, he mounts the marble pulpit steps.
'My dear boys, I want to tell you how I recall
one vivid evening in a tent in India...'
I allow the dogged tones bring into focus
memory's image, hold up compassion's looking glass
to read the mirror-written agenda of his words.
It seems the chapel has emptied, I listen alone.
He slopes forward with the weight of utterance, then
tosses back his head as though withdrawing all.
'Smirk if you will. A padre I staunched souls'
forebodings, shared tent and table with my troops,
rough-hewn men, salt of the earth, the Empire's
marrow. Smile, yet it wasn't easy to settle
to age in a draughty castle. Here might have been

the seedbed of Home Rule, our country's Eton –
forgive me if I sour, a fruit beyond its season –
instead this your mix 'em gather 'em state...'

But we are streaming up the aisles, another Sunday:
a brief pause and the great varnished doors
open to release the Hooley to the lions. A titter
darts through the congregation; all agog we watch
Father C. Gilhooly, bespectacled, a self-defensive pout,
tilting his left shoulder to trace some invisible
wall of support, in sheer spite of himself
the unerring clown: 'I was once driving in a car – '
The Hooley in charge of a car? Loud chortles.
'Actually,' he falters, 'I was driven by a woman...'
I hear our ridicule still echo down the chapel.
Bleed for him now a miscast man, remember
his moments busy in the hobbyroom or watercolourist
taking his clutch of favourites on nature walks.

Who is this hurtling through the doors, a fierce
energy swirling in the full skirt of his soutane?
Bugs O'Leary, Rev. Father Organiser of Almost
Everything, charmer of boys' sisters and mothers,
guardian angel to the nurse, prefect of the study-
hall where his thick soles creak on the parquet
as he spins accusingly: 'O'Herlihy, shut up!' –
his strange adenoidal bark plays a little
to the gallery. Now and again, breviary in hand,
he exits (a smoke on the side in the nearby bookroom).
Why do I always imagine him a benign *pater familias*
walking up an aisle giving away bride after bride?
Now enter Blacko, a bluff poseur, his profile
a fixed scowl. I watch him twitching at his collar:
'Damn it man, if you found a bicycle in a desert
you'd assume some originator' – proof by design,
as if proof were needed. 'So you know I was
here in your father's time,' he bawls at my neighbour.
'That's why I sometimes call you Andy!' Nothing
or little had changed; a sort of proof by stolidity.
The upholder of our equilibrium was happy in his heaven.
He readjusts his collar, marches across the sanctuary.

Four ghosts of old certainties forsake that altar.

Visit

Sunday afternoon about three o'clock
('with prior permission from your prefect')
pewed in a car on the gravel forecourt
our talk swivels between two worlds.
Angling herself in the passenger seat
my mother turns her face to me;
awkward behind a steering wheel, father's
eye catches mine in his rear-view mirror.

I rehearse this scene trying to read
my mother's face wondering if she sensed
I had left for good – son and emigré.
Four months' days ticked off a calendar,
at last I'd return a displaced guest
uneasy with neighbours, missing school-friends,
my eye proportioned to halls and arches
and home diminished as a doll's house.

Family doings, bulletins from a neighbourhood,
mention of names, small emissaries
of emotion from suburban roads, old
gravities draw me for a moment homeward.
And I resist. We are visitors for each other.
Unwittingly those weeks of initiation leave
a baffle between us. Our words fall short.
I am learning a new language, another lore.

Foster-Figure

Even now there is some enigma
in that glance. Though long grown
beyond a first self-surrender
or cooler reappraisals, I prize
his affirmation, always revere him.

Odd how I had found favour.
Did he know I craved the nurture
of his words? I fall on my feet:
prodigy, prize-winner, captain,
a protegé moving in his slipstream.

Surely among my fosterers
he laid the lightest of hands;
strings until then silent
in a father's shortfall of sanction
stirred, trembling toward song.

I probe the essence of this energy;
no blandishments or blind approval,
his unblinking trust enticed me,
fingered some awareness of worth;
in his praise all is possible.

Though at first a copy-cat tremor,
after many storms I'll still
strum the chord of his assurance,
that music I'll make my own,
an old resonance I'll summon up.

Shoulder-High

An image shapes those winter afternoons:
our breath plumes the frost as we drill
scrumming down over the stud-pocked mud.

A sweaty rapture heaves and shoves,
furies of willpower rise moonlike
in the mind and we bullock inches forward.

Faith in flawless moves, elusive flashes,
clay feet as light as angels' wings you race
and race and dream immortal touch-downs.

'Run it !' the crowd urged, 'run with it!' –
around men's jostling shoulders you'd glimpsed
a winger arcing inwards to the corner flag;

whistles, rattles, horns, coloured scarfs
flung in loops of glory, we'd stamped
as a train rumbled under the stand.

A thumping bell: *wumba, wumba, wumba*
ging, gang, shoulder-high down the marble steps
ride the conquerors. Three cheers for the captain!

Dusk. Like tap-dancers we clack the bootroom's
terrazzo, sit musing fleshy and happy
plucking soil from between the studs of our boots.

Fallen Angel

Returning another autumn we discover
a changed regime, a community reshuffled;
losing my sponsors in that shake-up,
roots too shallow, I fall from grace.

New brooms with fresh sweeps.
How easily we become how we're seen;
failure throws an oblong shadow,
I cover hurts with a jaunty humour,

pretend not to care, affect disdain,
harden the core to day-by-day
humiliations – tiny erosions of respect –
learn the slow rustings of shame.

And laugh a bitter laugh! while inside
discs of trust skew and warp.
Where can you turn? You've made your bed,
now lie there widower to your dream.

How many faces must a wound wear?
Iconoclast, windmill-tilter, self-saboteur,
stunted years of a poise too hard won;
yet in such moves the spiral turns...

Nothing. A squall in a child's cup!
But you're the child, this is your cup.
I own no master. My gods of innocence
fallen, I clench a fragile self-reliance.

Reverie

He must have seen in my make-up some countersign,
he must have seen me seeing him despising
demons of his childhood he needed to exorcise,
his own clumsy intensities mirrored in mine.

It seems he must have enjoyed my fall from grace;
a tap on the left shoulder 'Straighten that slouch!';
term reports: 'This boy daydreams far too much';
those constant small-time displays of O'Grady-says.

Friends stand by me. I bluster and swear
some day I'll tell him; we indulge the numb
reverie of revenge. In turn that day will come:
walking by a bus queue who should you see there...

There had been rumours of a breakdown. 'A hyper-active
temperament,' they said, 'poor Father Joe'. As I slip by
I catch that ageing man averting his nervous eye.
What ironies make a captor more victim than his captive?

Old Wine

Another October, middle-aged, black-dressed,
urbane. It will have been mid-June we last
shared refectory tables, years of crumbs
wedged in their grooves. Dream beyond terms,
hopes, fears, expectations. A quarter-century:
rub-a-dub and who do you think we'll be?

A stranger, a handshake, a name spoken.
Imagine swathes of hair, gawky enthusiasm.
Maybe it's the voice's fall I recognise?
How the mind plays tricks: mouth, eyes
begin to resemble memory turned hindsight;
this was the story to be, the face to fit

a brewer, a banker, a hotelkeeper. We swap
life-tales. (Will some shy away; black sheep,
the loners?) Five years apart for each year
I'd spent there. Some shaft sunk together
into our early earth, a corridor of fondness
moistens, wells. An old yearning openness.

'Are you happy?' I dare. 'Well maybe not
the way I'd dreamt, I just accept my lot.'
A face that suffered. Another recalls rivalry
others remember differently. Let it by:
nexus of myths, fictions to which we cling,
wine of fables spilt deftly on the tongue.

Blue cheese, swirls of cigar smoke and guffaws;
a toast, our madcap heckling, boisterous applause.
The past is present. Confirm me class-brother;
ghosts we tame and need or crave to lay together.
Addresses, promises and I'm full of at-one-ness,
of aloneness. Warmth flickers in a glass.

A Harsher Light

There we were, blazers and whites,
hands thrust in our pockets as we talked,
figures from a faded epoch that final
long summer term before the scattering.
Suddenly in the cram and grind of exams,
a hurried leavetaking and all was over.

Soon new realities are shaping.
Dumbfounded how readily we trusted,
took childhood's caste for granted.
We sort our memories, deftly rework
once certainties to mould conscious
visions of perfection, in hindsight

deplore that old man emptying slops,
our servant *Johnnies*, menial Brothers
(even in the graveyard serried *Paters*
and *Fraters* never mingled). At late-
night parties raising mugs of wine
we'll sing *There but for fortune...*

Bohemia, that counterworld is waiting,
unlatching its oyster of adventure; yet
entering the lonely labyrinth of choice,
for all the bravado, in spite of disavowal,
on the sly I rue the loss of an ordinance
open-and-shut, an inmate's bitter-sweet.

II. A BLURRED MUSIC

Come sarebbe belle il mondo
se ci fosse una regola
par girare nei labirinti.

How beautiful the world would be
if there were a procedure
for moving through labyrinths.

UMBERTO ECO

Youth

Break boyhood's taboo,
step on every line
to crack a devil's cup.
Hurts turn to arrogance.
We're naked and brazen
under the skies.

Our gods can wait.
No need to hurry.
Old wisdoms painfully unfold;
sooner or later
will we return, fumbling
from clue to clue?

Amazing how the gods
will choose to gamble,
hanging our destinies
on such flimsy plots
we stumble on a trail,
children on a paper chase.

Gestures, even intonations,
quirks of our childhood
heroes, once imitated
now become our own,
we stitch together
a patchwork of self.

Maybe some hints,
prompts from deities:
a word of praise,
spin-offs from mistakes,
strangers we met,
women who chose us.

Hearing the jazz of chance
we advance, making
headway by detour,
In such journeys subsist
the working of our karma,
the whirling of our stars.

Hesitation

The first awestruck flutter. To think
another cares! Promised phone calls,
letters in tinted envelopes, presents
swapped, delicacies of dress, faint
traces of *eau de Cologne*, a gentling
closeness; we nestled in such intimacies.

Meals *en famille*. A wealthy father
listens shyly to name-dropping, tiny
attempts at creditworthiness, while
mother bestows protective luxury;
allows a sort of ease by implication;
we are children playing house.

But something is sowing a doubtseed:
an instinct maybe or scapegrace need
to abandon shelter, stretch a wing,
perhaps a dream of an Eve *fatale*
who waits to bite a forbidden apple.
Must we lose the comfort of the garden?

Then those long spring evening walks;
wistful handholding, blushed words,
minor kisses in the porch, our dallied
goodnights. A last orchard tenderness
before passionate winds outside those walls
lift such timid blossoms towards pleasure.

Questing

A time for gaiety, a time to sunder
taken-for-granted gods, to flounder
or squander; a feckless valley-time
before we find a cause and climb
into the laps of countergods, a bizarre
time when in some Dublin bar,
arguing the toss as best one could,
we served our apprentice adulthood.

Till closing time we talked and talked;
the intellect now cock of the walk.
What does it mean? We interrogate
our unbringing, unravelling with apostate
zeal a web of code and token
and court our guilty ecstasy of broken
symbols, a dance along the precipice,
new and giddy pull of the abyss.

We leave carrying our parcels of beer;
across a sidestreet; someone for the sheer
hell heaves a brick at a windowpane –
we scuttle out of trouble down a lane

back to our meagre Bohemia to expound
meanings of the universe. Above the sound
of our voices a bedsitter radio is playing;
between stations, a blurred music sways.

Manhood

Soap the butts of the fingers, back straight,
knees bent, the shovel does the stooping;
whatever you do, keep scratching. The sagging
cement bag heaved from a shoulder thumps
dead-weight on the dust, its layered paper
slit across the belly-bulge by angled
jabs of our shovels, each half then
tugged apart. *So you'll never
go back now mate!* A bucket
swung by its handle, slops of water
puddle through grey powder, shovels
knead in the gravel, scooping, slicing.

Student? – the Clare ganger menaced
Jaysus no! Money, of course
(notes fanned and counted on a bed)
but more an expiation. Remember a first
shock hearing returned Araners
round on their children, shout in Cockney:
Shut your bloody mouths, wi' you!
Here they were in Pimlico. Blistered
palms atone for privilege, self-obliteration
mixing the powder with gravel. Back
straight, let the shovel do the bending;
scooping, slicing, working into one.

Out on top, you and the sledge –
orders from the ganger. Storeys up
jauntily astride a sheer wall
Blacks are billowing brick and dust.
One breaks this rhythm to watch
my unsteady hands measure timid

swings for the sledge. *Hey*, he hoots,
hey! you paleface is yella!
Below the ganger's arms beckon.
He rehearses a now ritual dismissal
(a nephew due next week from Clare)
You'll be finishing up tomorrow.

Friday at noon abandon duties,
search out another site, another
start. *Excuse me could you
please tell me where…* a bowler-hatted
man cuts a silent half-circle,
passes in disdain. Stung an instant –
a desire to pull rank, to rail,
tell him who you really are…And
who may I ask are you, sir?
Smeared with gravel and limestone
(insignia of reparation), human and alone,
scan that London skyline for a crane.

Spilling

Should we regret
our rush towards light?
Belligerent shoots of elder,

pimpled and taut, sun-
hungry jabbed upwards
through an old canopy.

Should we regret
a youth spent spilling
our bonebred innocence?

First water runs
through dry clay
yet trails of its moisture

Clot the porous soil.
Earth thickens to trap
its second innocence.

Reflection

Surely we fell for the self in the other,
our sweet will a mirror admiration;
fellows in intensity, our volatile attraction,
quick countersigns of likeness.

Fringe and lashes gleamed in laughter;
with swoops of black hair shoulder-length
she jutted her head rebelliously; behind
her jerky gladness a frailty lurks.

She stood on a table, sang *o rise
up lovely Sweeney*, every note
a theft, a spilt life – her nerves
spinning out that spalpeen's odyssey.

Under her command the room quivers.
(Did we fear for the spendthrift spirit?)
All in my youth and prime we drift
together *from the clear daylight till dawn.*

How blindingly we travelled. Confess
hindsight: maybe less love more desire,
a sullenness uncoiling moist and grateful.
'All my men were lonely,' she said,

'all my men were driven' – her generous
mandate to caress the loner, to tempt,
to take, to rock, to slack, to lull
a moment in forgetfulness. How blindingly

at one, at odds, our humours shuttled –
loving or rowing – forever caught
in ironies of likeness; a self-recognition
drawing us together, pulling us apart.

III. FISTS OF STONE

Was there ever a cause too lost,
Ever a cause that was lost too long,
Or showed with the lapse of time too vain
For the generous tears of youth and song?

ROBERT FROST

Wanderers

O saga of all that has happened
we know the tales and still
must we too be wanderers?

Gilgamesh strikes out for glory,
journeying to the Land of Cedars
to fight the giant Humbaba.

Redresser of wrongs, grasper
at golden shadows, Quixote
the knight is spurring his horse.

Is it then the same story:
a bid to shortcut history,
our scattergood craving for Eden?

Heroic or errant, do we loop
the loop or does goddess life
love the intensity of our tour?

Watch over us on our travels
o saga of all that has happened
if we must be such wanderers.

Stranger

A youngster I came, pilgrim to the source;
fables of a native bliss stirred mottoes:
A land without a tongue, a land without a soul.
As the currachs drew alongside the steamer
men in dark blue shirts shouted exotic words.

In the kitchen a daughter returned on holiday
switches from her mother's tongue to chide
her London children. As I listen it seems
I am foreign to both, neither fish nor flesh.
Was I to be a stranger in this promised land?

I slip into a glove of language. But there's still
a vividness, an older mood, small courtesies
to fortune: the sea must have its own – to swim
is to challenge fate. Child of reason and will
I am at most a sojourner in that mind.

Talk then of the mainland as *the world outside*,
enter and become a citizen of this stony room:
handkerchief fields claimed from rocks, dung
dried for fuel, unmortared boulder walls,
calfskin shoes, stark artifices of survival.

A widower welcomes my visits, opens his sorrow
to the incomer. Gauchely, I mention his loneliness:
Hadn't he his turn? ask two neighbour women
swirling in their petticoats *What ails him?*
they banter, standing in the sunshaft of a doorway.

One evening on the flags dancing starts up;
no music, island women summering from Boston
lilt reels, long to be courted. But men
shy of plaid skirts or lipstick don't dare
(still too boyish, subtleties pass me by).

Nudges and smothered laughter among the men.
Over again the word *stranger*. I bridle,
yearn to be an insider, unconsciously begin
a changeling life; turning a live-in lover
I wear my second nature, a grafted skin.

Folksong

The voice is the only music that says what it tells
When I go to the Lonely Well I sit and anguish...
A message stretching its tendrils to memory calls,

summons up echoes, as if the bereft – the vanished
or absorbed – are naming their ghosts, a medley
of losers: Picts, Mayas, tribes of the Suquamish...

The singer quavers out that one love's agony,
cranks its rhythms out of a neighbour's hand:
the undertwang of the music keeps shifting the story.

*The sap running in the pine carries the red man's
sacred meaning, the water's murmur is the voice
of his father's father; the white man takes this land*

but all things share the one breath. The poise
of the dispossessed freights and lifts the turns,
tuning each line to the same plaintive noise.

Will the stones remember their feet? the seabirds
claw ogham epitaphs in the wriggled sand?
The singer winds down to the final spoken words.

A loneness in the shaft of the song refuses to end.

Coastlines

A temperament takes on the world. I chose bleak
slabs of limestone, lone outcrops, promontories
poking their stubborn arms against an Atlantic;
supple elbows of strand seemed like cowardice.
Lines will blur, a seaboard fret and shift,
waves spending and being spent into the silence
of endless sands, rhythms of challenge and drift
husbanding or yielding the jigsaw shore of an island.
It's best the blue-grey rocks know nothing of how

constant water wears, a coiling uncoiling motion
flushing each snag or edge, ebb and flow
scouring the grain, their work being worked by ocean;
clenched fists of will jutted in their prime,
tangs of stone daring a tide or time.

Leavetaking

A moment balancing on a thwart,
then aboard the mainland steamer;
an islandman shook my hand,
laughed 'When you land, hide
all that Gaelic under a stone!'

His words echoed. All over
the earth people are drifting
on this tide towards amber lights:
cities stretch out arms in greeting.
These were the giants we'd fight.

Was this Sancho Panza gainsaying?
*Take care, your worship, they're
no giants but windmills, their arms
are sails whirled in the wind
to make the millstones turn.*

But his worship could not hear;
zeal has its own defences: I knew
while in Boston fellow-countymen,
still too close to feel safe,
had scoffed at his broken English.

I clung mulishly to that world;
with the strange infatuation of rebuff –
that half-caste love – I claimed
my membership. (Leaving the school bus
someone jibes 'There goes the patriot.')

Older I'd plead the cause:
an inheritance was sliding away.
If only I had been a treasurer
of fragments but all my youngness
willed that life to survive...

It was enough to love. We thought
the giants would fold their arms
and yield, as though nothing
could beat our stripling will:
youth and death were strangers.

Decades after in a city hospital
I interpret for an islander. (At first
they'd thought him deaf: nurses
enunciate loudly; sign and gesture.)
The touring matron halting a moment

on rounds, speaks her *cupla focal*
and reverts. A face lightens and darkens
inwards. And how many days more?
Would he have to return? I hear
humiliation fall like a millstone.

The steamer cranks its anchor in
swamping the last creaks of wooden
thole-pins. Black-tarred coracles
ride accusingly out of reach:
I wear the skin not the flesh.

Timepiece

Some gentleness seemed to mark her out among
the islanders. Days on end her talk mothered me.
Could I bring anything to thank her? I'd asked,
surely there was something she'd fancy? Childlike
in anticipation, pincering a thumb and forefinger
around her cuff, she'd mentioned a wristwatch.

I loved her toying delight as she watched
a golden arrow flicking its delicate seconds by.
A gift or a spoiling? Shudders of suburban grey,
the panic of clock-watching an unkillable time
counting down remorseless minutes, a millennium
of hours before a homecoming, turn of a latchkey.

There was, of course, the alarm with a yellowing face
and clumsy tick but mostly just her half-glance
at the angle of light in the door. Days tumble
into easy rituals, clearing of ashes, the thump
of sods in a bucket; even moments of gazing,
tiny flickers of meaning, fragments gathering.

I'd heard her tell the story of the sleeper's soul:
butterfly leaving his mouth to wander and return;
when he woke his dream had been the insect's journey.
Long afterwards a brain surgeon remarks how we explain
so narrowly, how maybe consciousness hovers beyond
the skull...Does history toss our loss and gain?

It will all happen so quickly, one decade
catching a few centuries of Europe's change.
Off-the-peg chequered jackets begin to break
the uniform bawneen; a new buzz of motorcycles,
electric light, a screen perched in the corner,
exiles with newcomer wives return to settle.

'To set the hands, pull and twist it here' –
I took for granted. Fingers never focused
on such smallness fumble about the winder.
Laughing aside the awkwardness, I take her wrist
where a tanned hand meets the white of arm
like a tide-mark, I tighten and buckle the strap.

In Memoriam Máirtín Ó Cadhain

Which face of many faces entranced
our fledgling time? Outsider
untamed and untamable, scorner of prudence,
blind and wide-eyed,
a hurt innocence striking out on every side.

Or was it a mirror-nature mothering
out stories to transcend
failure, lover of the blundering and the suffering
on this road without end,
a watching watchful eye stark and tender.

Those closing years, probing and embattled,
he sought somehow to wed
the avant garde with the vanishing, straddled
a destiny – a watershed,
new and old flirting and parting in that head.

Over Kirghiz, he broods as the engines swirled:
were high-haunched jets horses
riding to the Well at the End of the World? –
For no one knows
through what wild centuries roams back the rose?

The sweetsmelling heartbreaking rose.
He puzzles Oisín's tour to a zone
of youth, his touchdown to dust: 'Who knows
maybe they'd foreshown
Einstein's time moving in a chamber of its own.'

Or the gritty humour? When the hearse stalled
we hoisted you shoulder high
slowing a midday city to a crawl;
laughing nearby,
a spirit rode the white steed skyward.

I see you returning ten generations on,
defiant and full of youth,
demanding how three hundred years have gone.
Tighten the saddle-girth;
your foot must never touch our island's earth.

Visionary

What was it then, what commanded such ardour?
A scattering of lonely islands, a few gnarled
seaboard townlands, underworld of a language frail
as patches of snow hiding in the shadows of a garden.

But the dwindling were so living. In this wonderland
of might-have-been I fell for the rhythm, the undertone
of my father's speech, built a golden dream.
(As you dreamt that land was falling asunder.)

A world as it is or a world as we want it:
when to resist old fate's take-for-granted
or when to submit; had I known before I slid
into a snowy fantasy, a fairyland of squander...

Was it a lavishness, a hankering for self-sacrifice,
part arrogance, part the need of the twice
shy for a paradise of the ideal, pure and beyond,
where one man's will turns a hag to a princess.

Oh I was the fairy story's third son, the one
who, unlike his elder brothers would not shun
a hag by the roadside: surely I'd rub the ring,
summon a sword of light to slay the dragon.

Tell me now that land was a last outpost,
a straggling from another time no one's utmost
could save; the hungry beast of change roved
nearer, that vision was a ghost dance with the past.

Tell me now third brothers too have grown
older, have even learned to smile at highflown
dreams. Then tell me still somewhere in the thaw
a child is crying over a last island of snow.

Dark

When the God of childhood first fell
I tossed my hair over my shoulder;
there was a will, there was a way –
the sap rises, the tide fills
flushed with dreams of its own motion.

Now there's a will but no way
must the sky with all its stars
rest stoically on these shoulders?
Did Atlas, loser of a golden
apple, resign and turn to stone?

No, not stone. Most of all
I fear the half-measure of greyness.
I choose the dark (or does the dark
choose me?) I want to fall,
open a chasm black and deep.

I plunge into an anarchy of gloom.
Can it be that dark before it slumps
conceives a light, prepares in its ruin
the already and not yet, heaves
long rhythms of chaos and creation?

But dark is dark: saddle of nothing
riding black hogs to the abyss.
Travel velvet spaces of despair;
terror, like a dredge, is scooping
out a void for love's surrender.

IV. TURNS AND RETURNS

Dark dreams in the dead of night
And on the reckless brow
Bent to let chaos in,
Tell that they shall come down,
Be broken, and rise again.

EDWIN MUIR

History

And we keep beginning afresh
an endless history
as if this odyssey
had never happened before? Yes,

yes, ours was a spoiled generation
secure, even tepid
somehow untested –
no plague or war, torture or starvation.

Look how some were keeping faith
in a gulag while we
fumbled out our destiny,
walking our easy under-urban path.

So it wasn't their route (wince
at the thought). Still,
freedom was a crucible,
blundering chalkless tour in labyrinths.

Maybe we grope the same journey
scooping the oracular
in scandals of the particular
light we throw on some greater story.

Why does the word keep taking flesh?
O nameless dream
wild stratagem
wanting to shape our venture. O Gilgamesh

forever traveller, your myth brooding
in us, we grapple
with redemption's fable.
O Scheherazade healing a cuckolded king.

Belonging

A child wanders
beyond his father's living-room,
timorous adventurer.
Suddenly, bearings lost, he has begun to roam,
a lonely hallway of doors.

A young man flaunts
his loss of innocence, laughing off
the boy that once
didn't know a warm room was an alcove
walled in by his father's wants.

His years unwind.
A sceptic he scanned the doors and said
On the one hand
but then on the other. Lists of choices unmade.
What was it he didn't understand?

Was his wisdom
unlived in, second-hand experience
Of Peeping Tom
agog on every threshold, whipping his glance
between the frame and jamb?

Guarding his freedom
he shrugs if others pass through the door
of a chosen sanctum,
as though he doesn't know he's chosen a corridor,
this long and draughty room.

But still a question:
how, knowing every argument and angle,
to find a way in,
to tread wittingly over one door's saddle
into a room of belonging?

Underworld

Mid-morning. Beyond my blinded window
a day of creation is playing its show,
its theatre of noise. After elevenses
roofers hoist metal ladders against
a nearby gable, down a lane
children are chanting *cowardy cowardy
custard*; my neighbour must by now
be pegging her rainbow of towels on a line.

All day to do it and nothing done.
Three other books opened, begun
and abandoned; days of no purpose,
blank canvases, nadir of choices
unmade or deferred, nagging self-pity,
endless wavering and analysis. A scan
of newspaper columns fancies 'An Arabian
company requires a dynamic...(only

under twenty-fives need apply).'
Clock-watched hours weigh a century,
All day to do it and nothing done.
Is there nothing new under the sun?
Here is spiral of dark irony:
a dread of transience begins a despair
which in turn makes time unbearable.
Chaucer named *a synne of accidie*

this see-saw anguish: a thwarted will,
a clotted mind struggling to a standstill.
And meaning seizes up. *Dip your bread
in mustard* the laneway children said.
Are our days just moments that appear
and disappear or is every act heir
to an act and time that gathering river
where histories run? Wake up, sleeper!

I turn over, glazing my mind
with fragments. My tongue begins to thicken.
All the flow has gone to earth.
Ground waters stir underneath,
between soil and rock through sandstones
and shales a spring gargles against
a flag's stern underside. I dream
I'm shifting slabs from over a source.

Probing

And there is no knowing
the weight that weighed, the agony that drove
a mind beyond its edges. Although disavowing
daylight, was he still begging love
by that dark going?

A child, a vague
signal of trouble – a threat inbred –
his name had seemed charged with guilt by lineage:
'The eyes and temperament' they said
'his spitting image!'

A little older
I recall a visitor warm with charm:
'Remember I am both uncle and godfather'
he laughed, stretching a gentle arm
around my shoulder.

For years the same
lavishness: a windfall cheque 'just a token
of affection!' I'd almost forgotten the capricious gleam
in his eye when suddenly a broken
man came

flamboyant in despair.
I knew his moods, his jerky semaphores
of warning, struggled to answer 'What does it matter?',
strove vainly to hold doors
of trust ajar.

At first the narrow
seed of terror, a tribesman's fear,
such an end might coax their kin into a burrow
of dark; I'm afraid his ghost might steer
too near the marrow.

That blotting out
I search again, summon his generosity –
uncle and godfather remember! And did I doubt
the gentle arm stirring pity
like water in a drought?

An arm now cleaning
shafts, unclogging disused conduits,
compassion at such an exit probes an opening
in old wells; shared genes and spirits
cry out for meaning.

Our lives reverberate.
As though by proxy beyond the frontiers
I have visited the blackness of his forever night
and now return to double-live arrears
of fragile sunlight.

Vision

Hollowness of eyes with no
more tears; brittle vessel
that won't weep from its clay.

Imprints, traces, shadows
of all who suffered summon
my crying. Need into need.

Breakdown of self,
cleansing of sight,
watering to the roots:
oneness with everything.

High Tide

O goddess life, gather me into your flow!
White horses ride high into the taking shore –
who's winner, who's loser in such a love-making?
The mind resists a moment, hanging like a bird
caught in crosswinds. So this is high tide.
I wonder as I walk Bull Island's ribbon of sand
is this the morning Gilgamesh wept because a world
held back its secret *But be merry and make your bride*
happy in your embrace, this too is the lot of man.
A chaos of foam recedes, look an archipelago,
islands of froth dividing, a genesis in water,
creation's second day, a world reshaping!

Dunlins wheel in unison, fledgling consortium
snatching in their span plays of light's mystery,
they tilt out of dark undersides of splendour.
And still the earth melodeoned by the moon's
gravities moves a tide. Near the waterside
an old man sits to watch the sun's climb

to another summer; tumbling, tumbling in the dunes
tip and tig children still laugh and hide
in their laughter. *Is everything marvellous in its time?*
So who then can number the clouds in wisdom?
Goddess life sighs dizzily in her ecstasy –
'Love me!' I heave sweetly into our surrender.

Freedom

Enough was enough. We flew
nets of old certainties,
all that crabbed grammar
of the predictable. Unentangled,
we'd soar to a language
        of our own.

Freedom. We sang of freedom
(travel lightly, anything goes)
and somehow became strangers
to each other, like gabblers
at cross purposes, builders
        of Babel.

Slowly I relearn a *lingua*,
shared overlays of rule,
lattice of memory and meaning,
our latent images, a tongue
at large in an endlessness
        of sentences unsaid.

Those We Follow

The best said little, yet enough to signal praise
the best said least, never laid too heavy a hand;
just a glance of light, a path I might find,
but I followed false signs, stumbled into byways.

At last I retrace, begin the haul again –
the double task that probes the double faith of loss
before gain. And then a patient glow of progress.
I so wanted them to know, to call to them:

Oh, look what I have done! But they have gone
beyond the bend and out of sight. I sway
an instant, peering ahead; a voice resonates:
steady as you go, you carry someone's beacon.

Touchstone

Surely I'm not alone in this? Everyone
remembers some first fragrance – or was it
a colour or sound strumming the cranium?

My parents sat up night after night
to vigil my fever. Delirium and eternity
smudged into weeks I'd lie and wait,

gathering nerve for an August afternoon,
when at last I'm promised a whole hour
by my window, where the days still shone.

The curtains breathe an aroma of autumn.
The latticed speaker of a big orange-dialled
wireless croons and fills the bedroom.

Red gladioli rage busily in the garden,
blooming their loud swords, pickets
on paradise. It must have happened then.

And nothing else would ever do again:
blaze of an instant, infallible gauge
before we'd given it a meaning or name.

Or do some forget? Do some skate
easily along the rims of gloom?
Dark is darker after the light.

I crave take-off, long flights inward,
a glowing, height after height, hum
of a moment flown Icarusly near the sun.

Return

O river, indomitable woman
unearthing a course, a stubborn
momentum looping, your shovel
gouging by stealth; determined,
you scoop your bed – a lover
leaving no stone unturned.

I knew a half-bend of this river,
a slow arching of the Dodder
alongside a park-path between
two busy bridges, an elbow
of adventure where my Captain
Imagination sailed the Shenandoah.

School children had we begun
to gauge the swerve of wonder?
Who said truth was a fact?
The longest reach is the Nile:
somehow my Dodder contracted,
like a love not quite to scale.

Perhaps to know is to regain
the loss of gain, as when
he knew each loop and eyot
Twain mourned for mystery:
turning master and pilot,
had he lost his Mississippi?

In the same September sun
I skim a sliver of stone,
to count in water ricochets
decades now worn older:
I unwind into come-what-may,
an Atlas untensing his shoulders.

Is this then the return?
But the river hurries on.
No regrets. Wherever a curve
wanders at large, her waters
close up a hoop, cutting off
ingrown meanders of remorse.

O mover, driver of water,
channel of unplanned demeanour,
beautiful rover, you wriggle
of river, my Dodder of youth,
endless hunger for the possible
living from source to mouth.

V. REROOTING

This is travelling out to where

a curved adventure
splashes on planes of sunlight to become
one perfectly remembered room...

ANNE STEVENSON

Journeys

Does something mischievous scheme to leave
an infinity in each face of a single muse?
Does a man know every woman since Eve
travelling the ring of one lover's moods?
Maybe we choose a point to enter
the circle; then slant our painstaking
angle, a slope to the flaring centre,
a focused abandon, a slow love-making.
Strange, at the rim it seemed we left
a whirl of choices beyond recall;
in the hub's flush all angles met,
a needle-point where winner takes all;
a wheel is the rim of many ways,
spokes of intensity, journeys to the blaze.

Beginnings

A wing stirs in its sheath. Now it seems
all the fumblings of the larva years prophesied
this moment; under a crust our dreams
uncurl, eager again to dart and glide.
Still the giddy phase before the flight
when the gravity of self holds a little back;
once bitten, twice shy, we just might
dally in our shell, a last minute back-track.
All or nothing. We shed our last alibi
as when the insect nymph dares to prize
open unwanted skins, love's dragonfly
stretches its veinlike wings into the sunrise.
Two wings interlocked, the flight begun,
a speck of news flickers under the sun.

A Presence

Idle with pleasure, I let my misty gaze
find its slow way through the subdued
light to where the contour of a porcelain vase,
busy in silent meditation, alludes to you.
Along the dressing table a ceramic bazaar
of creams, moistures, lotions, ointments,
an exotic row of shapely pots and jars
stoppers the scents and vapours of a presence.
Your spirit travels in such lovely earthenware,
at ease in its clay, a vessel well turned,
cajoling the mind down from a castle in the air
back to the sweeter givenness of your world.
Still, like a wooer on his first sightseeing,
I relish the emblems, your haberdashery of being.

An Unfolding

An eager new shoot, I brimmed with sunkissed
boyish dreams of where my years might glide,
little knowing how a bitter frost could decide
the date of flowering, our story's turn and twist.
Damage done, the self – that secret strategist –
staunched its wound, anguished out of bruised pride
visions of Utopias, worlds cut and dried.
The heart, a frosted bud, tightened like a fist.
Your love – though it disclaims what it achieves –
unclenches me, keeping a watch, loyal yet unblinking,
full of yeses, fresh starts or that silent act
of merely being easy and ample as a mid-spring
coaxing open the horse chestnut's sweet smelling bract
to lodge sunlight deep in the fabric of its leaves.

Squall

A misunderstanding we should but didn't broach
rankles, then flares; one loaded remark
rocks our world. Strangers, we stand stark
and alone as words sweep us in whirlwinds of reproach.
Old sores glare. Once more the soul's search:
why did we risk the naked light or embark
on this journey? Yet why forestall dark with dark?
Buffeted we ride the storm's pitch and lurch.
A squall clears, the sky lifts – our kisses
timid tokens of amnesty as the purged air
breathes its sweet aftermath. Diffident, we pledge
never again like fledgling lovers still aware
how the great fluke of love poises on a knife-edge;
even the turning earth trembles on its axis.

The Other Voice

You came lean and taut, a barrage of innocence.
I remember a bluster of haughtiness hiding a boy
still dazed with childhood hurts, a man tense
with desire; slowly I thawed and rocked you in joy.
You mocked our speck of being; I showed instead
of dust a galaxy whirling in the sunbeam's eye;
you cried at the size of eternity, I hushed and said
eons count as kisses under a lover's sky.
No half-measures then. I have made this island
of life a kingdom. Have I stinted your ease
or pleasure? No, how could a woman understand
that men still talk of freedom to go as they please?
My love is your freedom. Do or die or downfall,
it's all or nothing and I have chosen all.

Out of the Blue

Nothing can explain this adventure – let's say a quirk
of fortune steered us together – we made our covenants,
began this odyssey of ours, by hunch and guesswork,
a blind date where foolish love consented in advance.
No my beloved, neither knew what lay behind the frontiers.
You told me once you hesitated: *A needle can waver,*
then fix on its pole; I am still after many years
baffled that the needle's gift dipped in my favour.
Should I dare to be so lucky? Is this a dream?
Suddenly in the commonplace that first amazement seizes
me all over again – a freak twist to the theme,
subtle jazz of the new familiar, trip of surprises.
Gratuitous, beyond our fathom, both binding and freeing,
this love re-invades us, shifts the boundaries of our being.

St Brigid's Cross

All business, a sheaf of rushes cradled carefully
in your arms, a culotte swaying daylight in your stride
you hurry indoors to set about a February ceremony
shaping your namesake's token, flourish for Spring's bride.
A city child, I'd seen the crosses above doors but missed
this rite, so it always seemed that something in the stretch
of those curious jerky arms with bows on their wrists,
honey-coloured and brittle, beckoned to a world beyond reach.
Lank green stalks crisscross their sign language;
seasons of hands are working that saint's emblem,
a lineage moving in your fingers; instinctively you bridge
worlds kneeling on a Dublin floor to knot a rush stem.
I watch you weave as the rush twists and reappears
a fresh-cut badge of love, this nexus of our years.

While You Are Talking

While you are talking, though I seem all ears,
forgive me if you notice a stray see-through
look; on tiptoe behind the eyes' frontiers
I am spying, wondering at this mobile you.
Sometimes nurturer, praise-giver to the male,
caresser of failures, mother earth, breakwater
to my vessel, suddenly you'll appear frail –
in my arms I'll cradle you like a daughter.
Now soul-pilot and I confess redemptress,
turner of new leaves, reshaper of a history;
then the spirit turns flesh – playful temptress
I untie again ribbons of your mystery.
You shift and travel as only a lover can;
one woman and all things to this one man.

Hindsight

Though thankful, at first finding the glare too bright
I flinched – as when the long-sought sun comes,
shrivelled by too much winter, the core numbs;
timorous in the glow – a sudden bout of stage-fright.
But it's all summer now. Your lavish sunlight
wakes and stretches these Van Winkle limbs;
I nuzzle up to the warmth, the love-sap brims
over, plush with the freedom of second sight.
Yet sometimes across the moon sky a sullen
cloud laments those angry years – hauteur
of hurt – when spring slid without my noticing
the willow covers its blossoms with silver fur,
as hedge-sparrows flirted and jerked their wings
and the east wind scattered the alder catkin's pollen.

A Circle

After lights out, weary from the long regime,
remember the dressing gowns, the illicit tiptoe
to whisper at the radiator hugging its last glow
until nabbed by the flashlight's accusing beam.
The first Christmas break passed in a daydream,
the rooms dwarfed, home become a side-show
to a cosmos of corridors and braggadocio, as though
the garment of childhood had slit along its seam.
Now I love to watch the lighthouse at Howth
flash its codes to steer ships past our gable,
to gossip in the dark with you my bed and boarder
and marvel at how, like tortoises in an Aesop fable,
our years have coiled their slow circles of growth;
a world brought back to scale, a house to order.

VI. OPENING OUT

The sun! The sun! And all we can become!
And the time for running to the moon
In the long fields, I leave my father's eye;
And shake the secrets from my deepest bones...
            THEODORE ROETHKE

Disclosure

Remember how at school we folded and unfolded
sheets from a jotter, scissored chunky *m*s and *n*s,
a saw-edge,
a clump of paper squared, melodeoned.
Then delight as it reopens
a fullness of design, transfigured wounds
unfolding in a page
berries, acorns.

The moment's contours scatter in the light.
A crossbeam gathers in pattern and fringe,
traces of passion,
hologram of thought, memory's freight
until a beam re-throws the image,
an intensity unpacking stripe and whorl;
each fraction
an implicit all.

Acorns of memories, berries of dreams.
Does every pilgrim's tale sleep in one moment?
Some inbred
whole uncodes in a tree's limbs,
spreads in slow workings of environment.
Soil, air, water, sun quicken
a word in the seed.
Time thickens.

Grantchester Meadows

Across Grantchester Meadows, May has snowed
cow parsnip, hawthorn, chestnut; a stone's throw
from here the Cam grooves slowly towards King's.
An English heaven: 'My real life began since
I came to Grantchester. I eat strawberries and honey.
A perfectly glorious time. Think only this of me.'

I see you Rupert Brooke blazered, flannelled,
a strolling presence in this albescent funnel
of young summer or picnicking under an oak
with Darwin's granddaughters: 'We used to talk
wearily about art, suicide, the sex problem.'
Übermensch, libido, absinthe, fin de siècle.

A 100 rings in an oak which may have seen
George Herbert brooding by the *Came* or Milton
explaining the ways of God now Galileo's sun
no longer danced attendance on our world. Newton,
did you some midsummer hatch along this path
laws to bring our universe back to earth?

'Certainly I approve of war at any price,
it kills the unnecessary.' Evenings of tennis
and cricket. It's the Aegean 1913:
'My poem is to be about the existence of England.'
Dead before the Dardanelles. A circle closes;
the hawthorn almost in bloom, the oak leafless.

Wars. Disillusion. Certainty a fallen idol,
our daylight turns a dice-dance of potential.
Turmoil of change as an old order dies
into us. Herbert must have known the crux.
Does the slow-leafing oak trust without proof?
I know the ways of learning yet I love.

Ghost Brooke you could be my father's father,
yet I'm your elder. Ride my Aeneas shoulder
as Grantchester blooms a lover's carte-blanche,
another innocence. Do you remember how strange
the fullness of the riddle seemed? *The acorn can't
explain the oak, the oak explains the acorn.*

Motet

O my white-burdened Europe, across
so many maps greed zigzags. One voice
and the nightmare of a dominant chord:
defences, self-mirroring, echoings, myriad
overtones of shame. Never again one voice.
Out of malaise, out of need our vision cries.

Turmoil of change, our slow renaissance.
All things share one breath. We listen:
clash and resolve, webs and layers of voices.
And which voice dominates or is it chaos?
My doubting earthling, tiny among the planets
does a lover of one voice hear more or less?

Infinities of space and time. Melody fragments;
a music of compassion, noise of enchantment.
Among the inner parts something open,
something wild, a long rumour of wisdom
keeps winding into each tune: *cantus firmus*,
fierce vigil of contingency, love's congruence.

Train Journey

As a boy I was sure that the track's anapaest
kept narrating each passenger's tale: like a charge
of experience, each face was a secret released.

Soon we rushed over a bridge's trestled brick-arch,
almost loving the dare and danger of a fall
till the train suddenly hurtled into shafts of dark.

Who would make it through this funnel
of night? Was it too long to believe
light might be waiting in the eye of the tunnel?

Some would go under in the dark. I grieve
for a fellow-traveller, a woman taut
as a violin, lavishing her girth of life

into song. Too near the edge and overwrought:
But how should I sing unless I burn?
Long afterwards I'd discover she'd fought

to the death her loneliness, flitting in turn
from friend's door to door. If I'd known
could I have comforted her? Was our sojourn

together a barrier to an inaccessible zone
of once intimacies? Always I remember
a voice spilling *from clear daylight till dawn.*

Like a child half awake on a morning in mid-summer
I'm rubbing the dark from my eyes. Unbelievable
how the light is dispatching its trees like ambassadors

that glide by our windows with an urgent epistle.
And I think I then knew that a train's undersong
began mourning the traveller whose story I'd tell.

Kinsmen

Father used to love to walk the block on Sunday;
skipping along a garden wall I found a slot
where our street met the road. 'The builder forgot
a brick' – my father shrugged but I insisted why?

Why? Why did that builder leave such a hole
just where our street met with the main road?
Why didn't Father know why? Through childhood
I am sure I puzzled over that slit in a wall.

Then I must have forgotten. Nearing the age
he begot me I think I heard someone explain
how the Hopi gathered their older children
in a hut to watch the gods' arrival in a village.

Painted ogres would circle, dance and howl,
then entering the hut they unmasked to expose
fathers and kinsmen playing at being gods.
I began remembering a peep-hole in childhood's wall

before the anger of disenchantment, before the flood
of our arrogance had swept both wall and garden.
So often since I have wanted to beg his pardon,
or at least to say how now I maybe understood.

Lately strolling the block again together
I asked nudgingly if he remembered that hole?
But he stares: 'Son, I am growing so forgetful!';
I fumble to link his arm, my ageing brother.

Matins

Segovia, guitarman, I know your prayer:
never mind, Lord, treasures laid up,
leave me this street where a greengrocer
draws a striped awning over his show
of yellow buttocked melons and blowzy peaches.

I can idle here by the corner, watch
children busy chalking a hopscotch
on the pavement or eavesdrop on schoolboys
bragging and smoking by the railway
bridge where young executives scurry.

A very ordinary mortal I gaze
boyishly at women's turquoise rings
as their hands touch in talk, delight
in loose cottons, linen blazers,
perfumes hugging air as they pass.

O polyphony of being, doing, bliss.
My senses feast. I breathe and am.
O hankerer after the irrevocable.
O plucker at words, colours, chords.
Are they real? Do we dream it all?

Gilgamesh, Odysseus, Mad Quixote,
wanderers relive in us your daylight.
And hey! what stranger down the line
moves to this rhythm, whose moment
twangs in the blood? Good morning, Segovia.

Perspectives

1

Like pegs, our forearms held the skein's coil.
Arcs of the knitter's hand unloop
and ball by turn. Sweep and detail.
A feeling of beginning in childhood's wind-up
I keep on recalling. Somehow I'm between
a yarn uncoiling to a tight ball of destiny,
a ball unravelling back the promise of a skein.
Plain stitch and design, point and infinity.
Who changes the world? Oh, this and that,
strands as they happen to fall, tiny ligatures,
particular here-and-nows, vast loopings
of pattern, the ties and let-gos of a knot,
small X-shapes of history; our spoor and signature
a gauze of junctures, a nettedness of things.

2

Whose music? A quiver enters like a spirit,
a murmur of tension from and back
into space. A tune of trembles in catgut.
The pride of an instrument as at its beck
and call the heart vibrates: pulse-sway,
dominion of rhythm, power before the slack
and silence. 'Pride before a fall' we say,
sic transit...Should we've been puritans,
taut, untouchable, our unshakable self-mastery
a vacuum of muteness? O noise of existence
shake in me a tone you need; sweet
friction of rosin, play me limp or tense.
Possessor of everything, owner of nothing.
Whose bow shivers its music in my string?

132

3

Nineteen forty-three, Tegel prison, Berlin.
I picture a face superimposed on a grille:
first widening of a smile, the mooning hairline,
something plump and composed, relentless will.
Time-servers slide; many in their armchairs
rage. Call them opters-out or captives.
Success makes history, I hear him say, *There's
no out. How will another generation live?*
The question echoes on: yardstick of ambition,
our spirit-level. Hanged Flossenbürg camp,
April of forty-five. Dietrich Bonhoeffer,
Like an eavesdropper, I glean smuggled wisdom.
Sometimes, it was piano wire – slower than hemp.
Suffer them in the light of what they suffer.

4

Specky-four-eyes, carrots, fatso, dunce!
Jeer and name-call and how we changed it to sport,
swagger of couldn't-care-less: *Sticks and stones
may break my bones, names 'll never hurt.*
But still he's there, that curly headed boy
scrambling a pillar: *I'm the king of the castle*;
a shout of territory, the old pedestal cry
defining by rivalry. *Get down you dirty rascal.*
Always black and white. Why south, why north,
pale-face or nigger or prod? I, Paddy,
dream the schoolroom globe, a balloon viewed
with a spaceman's floating glance; my heady
vision a sea with tatters and patches of earth,
our odds and ends hung on a line of latitude.

Memory

Again a silent room.
Doubt bows the cello
of morning. A diminished chord.
Lord Shallot to his loom
spelled to watch the river
in a mirror?
Why? While people war?
While people famish?

All the suspicions, excuses.
Where's the extravagant stillness
of a lover's mind?
Alert as madness, fierce
sojourner in a small womb's
patience. Then slowness:
rhythmic openings and closings
of woof and heddle.

Warped threads of memory
dream a weft, a journey
of doing – triple interplay.
Am I warden of filigrees,
patterns, the colours and plot,
keeper of the cloth,
the bobbin's eye, a forethought
in the shuttle's long cast?

Not even to try. A texture
of knots and intersections,
a youth ravelling its fulness,
layered music of complexity.
Cypresses sway in their spring;
the lattice and web of things
a frail morning
eastering another garden.

And the river moves:
a light, a shape, a weave.
Someone was busy in a kitchen,
someone was patching a roof,
someone was sowing wheat
or hustling the market.
Who was it noticed and forgot?
For us I've remembered.

Child

It's evening as I pass the first garden
a day's playthings scattered in the dew:
an upturned tractor yellow and forgotten
under lupins and London pride, a blue
rubber ball wobbled to a standstill.
Did someone call 'Come on, come on
it's bedtime!' And did you stall
the lone moment of sleep, of abandon?

I know your player's garden in
and out. Behind a fence and walls
silent first growths are gathering
sap in the long uncurling falls
of a dusk. Innocent know-how
is not to know. Beyond this greenroom
there are ordeals of suspicion. I know
the rip, the pain before bloom.

This take-for-granted is your garden.
Sureness of path, stakes and wires
that hold the sweet-pea, our heaven
of invention, dream-castle of desire.
Doubts are jags of bottle glass
on an orchard wall-top. Bit by bit
you awaken, must learn to mistrust
these gates your father shuts at night.

An apple-bite and that garden vanishes
forever. You too will roam with Adam.
Sap in the trees' limbs still lavishes
memories. You grow to another millennium.
Is what we love what we find?
Is there somewhere a second garden,
an arbour where the quickened mind
soars between its knowing and abandon?

Will the stars you once thought your own
slide infinitely away; mischievous,
faster-than-light teams of subatoms
conspire beyond your common sense;
a universe of unfoldings and enfoldings
draw in its mystery? Part and parcel
as housekeeper not householder
will you dream, fumble with the possible?

A dangerous growth. Make or break
a lupin slits its tight-lipped calyx,
London pride is living off its luck,
a rubber ball circles dark in itself.
Double-edge of nurture, of damage.
There's no undoing all our knowledge.
Bon voyage! Where will you choose
another garden, another innocence?

THE MIDDLE VOICE

(1992)

Three Rock

1

I stare from a dormer into the morning.
A line of hip-roofs, trees and then
the smooth curves of Three Rock Mountain.

How did it all happen? For years
I carried a poem I thought would begin:
'Now that I'm young, I want to say...'

The last of our parents' crowd stoop.
Friends' daughters are almost women.
My jet hair flickers ribs of grey.

Instead here I am saying it's good
to stand in between, touching our coming
and our going. Hinge and middleman.

The mast on Three Rock glints in the sun.
Receiver and sender. A signal boosted
onwards. Pride and humility of a medium.

2

I open a window and there's a dandelion's
grey head, a seed-parachute drifting
to a future on small breezes of obedience.

How will it all happen? That strange
floating openness. A trust. A patience.
One weekend a laboratory assistant

forgets a window; a mould wafts
onto a plate of microbes and invents
Fleming's penicillin. A leap of chance.

On dull mornings Three Rock vanishes.
Is there a mast picking up our signals?
I cling to a moment seized in its glint.

Eleven leap years. I begin to grasp
what the stare of a greying psalmist meant:
I will lift mine eyes unto the hills.

Arrival

Sweet dreams, Rebecca!
Snug with milk, unfussed
by toys or tinsel, not yet
six weeks beyond the womb,
stranger, you still trust
the eastern star that beckons
towards the manger of sleep.

Goodnight, newcomer –
while all the merry gentle-
men romp about the town
to pack the smokey inns,
down the season's compliments,
sing and warm their bones
around the bowl of fellowship.

All's well, my baby!
Adam model two
swaddled in his stable
sleeps deeply, so you
breathe easy as the donkey
whose breath puts out
an angel's flaming sword.

Goodnight, my girl!
Somewhere in the small hours
years ago another child
uncurls, hurries to discover
at the bed-end wisemen's gifts,
frets and begs the light
unfurl a paradise of day.

Sleep long, my lovely!
It's December – Jerusalem
light years away. We bow
between our thanks and trust
and so re-enter, what you
Rebecca still remember:
Eden of the eternal now.

Departure
(in memory of Máirtín Ó Direáin)

Autumn afternoons when time has weight
and shadows dip a balance towards the past
now even you must use that wicket gate
through which a memory sometimes slips a ghost.
My friend, I know just the way you'll come;
mourning spring in the west, alone and glum.
Then coaxing I'll ask 'How goes the hereafter?'
Are the women as lovely? Stabbing at solemnities
until we manage to tease
from you a final and knowing flicker of laughter –

'See that coin: heads we're here,
tails we're gone!' Cureless and endured,
a stoical pride grey and forlorn
as endless crags of his childhood Aran.

Scars of poverty became a lifelong
doubt; poems gallant and headstrong
thrown like small feudal bridges
of distanced trust, a troubadour's message.

His balm was always words and women.
He'd told me once he was smitten
by a face in the street, how he made her
his muse. A last courtly lover.

– I'll remember on a dying countenance as we crouched
over a spirit sighing still in its shell;
near the end bereft of words we touched,
laying palms on your forehead, took farewell,
abandoned your room. Outside was spring in the east;
your brow of fever still clammy in my fist,
as I gripped the hammer's haft, began to staple
a trellis to stay March's first caress,
fresh tendrils of clematis
unfurling trust in clefts of a pebble-dash gable.

Voices

1

From nowhere the Liffey estuary is spanned
by rainbow, a flyover of lensed sunlight
earthed in both its beginning and its end,
this voyage of a spectrum, arc of a flight

vivid and full. From where I stand
our house is in line with the bow's apogee.
It's almost as if I could stretch a hand
to either end. Shades of young Shelley.

I shrieked and clasped my hands in ecstasy.
The arch fades in the drizzle like a myth
Dear, and yet dearer for its mystery.
This middleness. My watch under the zenith.

2

First a ring to my mother to ask what I'd like.
Then, pigskin gloves, cuff-links, a tie-pin,
Anything a boy couldn't be seen dead wearing.

As I grew this would be our annual skirmish.
Finally, my twenty-first. A suitcase too big,
cumbersome and soon outmoded. 'Enough music

and books. He needs something solid to remember
his godmother with.' So maybe everything had
to be steady and tangible. A girl made good.

Grandfather treated her to holidays, a companion
for his only child. When she fell on her feet,
mother had bridled. Bittersweet. Love-hate.

'Who laid her out?' she demanded that morning
rearranging mother's last coiffure. 'Now,
she looks herself. There's the Eileen I know.'

This afternoon a voice crackles down the line:
'No happy returns. Don't you know I'm eighty.
I thought you promised to come and see me?'

3

But I have another call to make. 'I'm six'
a voice announces. Today is a birthday party.
Like names of reels, her blow-by-blow litany:
Hunt-the-slipper, Simon says, Hide-and-seek.
Out of nowhere a sunburst of breathless facts
about the colours and layers of her party frock.

We're talking long-distance. Timbres of each word
hoop through a satellite bowing the firmament
but we struggle with accents. I recall we scanned
favorite names guessing a gender in the womb.
And if it's a girl: *Rebecca Ford, Rebecca Ford.*
I'd imagined a strange intonation. 'I *am*, I *am*,

I *am* six,' she sings with delight. A conscientious
godfather, I've sent a gift-token but wonder still
should I have chosen. A god now doubting free-will,
I hear her listing presents. Already she's anxious
to return to play. A nexus of imperatives and chance
await: *pass-the-parcel and ring a ring o' roses.*

4

Two voices on a November afternoon
draw me into their presence;
a strange vibrancy summons,
shatters the present into a time unknown.
A configuration of moments seems to gather:
an outreach of arms, an odyssey
transcending a handclasped ecstasy,
a self loosening to the voyage of another.
Beyond the bowed colours the raindrops disperse,
Do my outstretched hands tip the ends of a universe?

142

Blemish

How exactly it happened? Which generation?
Just something my parents seemed to mention
and veil again. A stain on the imagination,

a seeping of words: 'recluse', 'disfiguration'.
Brothers jostled with a sister who'll stumble
on the hearth. Then, a habit and wimple

to conceal her scars. Proud and humble,
via dolorosa of a girl's about-face.
A closed order. My tomboy and anchoress.

A life left hanging in an air of disgrace
plays with the fire of a child's mind.
So young a woman immured and disciplined.

I wonder if a slowness of time refined
a suffering, her long self-forgetfulness
travelling some infinite kingdom of service.

Her presence still dips and surfaces.
A doctor describes a congenital syndrome:
'murmur, high mouth and dimpled sternum,

that temperament.' I hear the giddy drum
of the heart as she fell. In a niece's goodbyes
some frailty again wakens the memories.

Our storyline: dowries of Xs and Ys.
Suddenly, from behind a cowl of years,
who knows who's blooming a gene of hers?

A flight becomes a call and the stairs
of retreat now wind our endless wish.
I tread perfections of a healing blemish.

The Builder's Men

Today the builder's men are scaffolding a gable.
Mortar has weathered, the brick might be unstable
And the whole frame begin to sag. Through
An open window the boom of their voices renew
A house's dominion. They climb a crib of iron bar
And space, chisel and trowel our wear and tear.

'Look, Baba window!' prompts a mothering voice.
'Look!' he mimics and splutters arrays of noise
And wonder. 'Cooey!' calls the builder's man
Appearing and hiding at the window. 'Where's he gone?'
A little bewilderment before the sudden chortle,
Skips of delight. 'Where's the man with the trowel?'

Such amazing words! *the man, the trowel, the window*
Namings unravelled from the past that echo and echo
Saxon serfs and Normans, the scribes, the courtiers,
Puritans and frontiersmen, all owners and heirs
To a house of meaning they built and so abandoned,
Its well-worn brick now pointed in a child's astoundment.

A playpen made of sounds, gift and encumbrance
Of the past. But look! he almost seems to dance
To rhythms of syllable and scraping trowel, to begin
A long gurgle of conversation with the self. Then
Distracted, he gazes at the window we've left ajar,
The light flushed down the builder's house of air.

Tradition

A feeling of passivity, of handing over.
All that was received I again deliver

by just being here. Available. No more.
A watch of dependence, complete exposure,

not even trying not to try to achieve.
This work is a waiting, almost as if

a host, his palms held up in supplication
between two guests, begins an introduction:

'For years I've wanted you two to meet.'
The middle voice fading as they greet

in the sweet nothingness of a go-between.

Nakedness

1. *Shying*

As I move towards the centre,
an old temptation to shelter,
a need to shirk any danger.
to close up, to shut down.

An unscorched wallflower I'd sit
tight. A clammed spirit.
And why should I step it
out in all my nakedness?

That unnerving gladness,
the dance swaying its labyrinths
so full of sweet promises.
Oh, the flaming sword at its hub!

2. *Hurt*

Your music took me by surprise; nothing
by halves, I matched you move for move,
I warmed, I opened, I yielded, I loved.
You of all people to double-cross!

Is it anger that stings or is it shame?
Intimacy cuts both ways: I'd mapped
your nakedness: do I pay you back
(that way you'd have called the tune)

or withdraw, wear an aggrieved look,
sullen air of those who finding the world
guilty, seal off all the risks, turn
deaf ears to buffeting moods and rhythms?

Against the beat, between the throbs,
our moments leap and fall, jazz
notes of ecstasy, random arabesques
of anguish, a hazardous melody of being.

I reeled with pain, half anger, half shame;
reckless, over again, I gave everything.
Twice shy, I know I must curb the swing,
I know that I must watch my step.

But I know that I know nothing.
All that is certain is change. I plan
to gauge every footfall, but in the dance
my steps grow wide-hipped and lavish.

3. *Again*

The finesse of rebeginnings! Here like a novice
I seem to thrill at every spendthrift word
as we dispense ourselves in flares of newness.

We angle between a coyness of once intimates,
stiffness of half-strangers, allow our dead
image of each other quicken and become.

There have been so many dreams and stumbles,
infinitesimal shifts, inches of slow growth,
all our moves to make the same so different.

I hankered after you. Despite our separate
ways, our trade in coolness, somehow the flame
abides, sputters between desire and memory.

146

I confess my need to trim the blurred wick.
I love the thrift of shared ground, returns
to older trust, subtle closures of rift.

Hurt, jealousies, misunderstanding or drift?
Let's say it was a silence where we hoarded
the sealed years of business we now swap.

Wait! Supposing, how can we now be sure?
I shy from fire. You insist I drop veil
after veil; we stand before the naked flame.

A Toast on the Eve

Where is the star that winks in the east?
In this the nadir of the year, we sense
The drag of time. For a while deceased
Friends trouble us – a glum roundabout
Of memory. O beg a freshborn innocence,
Some star to blink beyond a doubt.

Where is the star that signals in the east?
Tonight I am both adult and child;
I shape and plan and still am an unleased
Tenant of my clay, never master of my history.
Ambitious and humble, I am reconciled
To bear this double witness to a mystery.

Where is the star that beckons to the east,
That God come down to bless the flesh
Of living? O give us the daily yeast
To burble through the veins and charm
Our sour grapes into wine. Find me the crèche
Where a god is cradled by woman's arm.

Where is the star that dances in the east?
Son of ghost and virgin forgive our meagre
Welcome. Busy in the inns, we feast
Your arrival cribbed between ox and ass.
O give us our innocence, all green and eager.
To a god of renewal, I raise this glass.

Rondo

Again that gangly earnestness
'Actually here's another I drew'
as I admire, dreamily a question:
'You know that painter you knew,

had he a studio?' a quaver
in the tone triggers my subconscious:
I too am twelve, all eager;
a bearded artist primes a canvas.

I watch, gauche with enquiry.
'O no!' he said, 'my father
disapproved but when he died
I found my notices neatly folded

in his wallet, the good words
circled in red' – a posthumous
boost filling those voids,
years of unworded praise.

'Where was his studio?' A rondo;
now it's my turn to respond,
conscious that each syllable
may float a seed in the wind:

'On the seafront, so he saw
each morning a northern headland,
for years just kept drawing
that line in every weather.'

Is this the thrill of lineage?
I grow young in your ardour;
then crossing too soon your bridges,
fear those agonies in the garden.

You nod, frowning a little;
lightly the talk changes course.
I pretend not to notice the first
tremble of manhood in your voice.

Largesse

The generous sink into traces they leave in us,
In tiers of personality, gestures, words we use,

Flashbacks to small confirmations, that hand lain
On a shoulder. The generous are still a glow within.

Confident, they knew nothing diminished their glory,
As they nourished seeds to flower for a while in me.

The jealous I begin to forget, frightened spirits
Nipping the bud of younger and younger threats.

The turning-point and I face both ways like Janus.
Recall how terribly you needed praise. Then choose.

Wavering

What sort of a country! Damn it,
a man standing for his father's seat.
Objectivity – I fumed. His eyes glaze,
as he points to a few roods of clay:
'You see that field? When I'm gone,
even the worms belong to my son.'

I thought of our quarrel today as I strove
to countersign cheques identically above
as below. Too full of exuberance, I turn
my letters boldly; they sag when I'm down.
Sometimes I slant an efficient miniscule,
then, the bank-girl smiles and I wobble.

So quickly our habit changes. A span
of school years and with ease children
talk in grammes and metres. Dream
of screens and dials, charm of system,
hunger for a norm, passionate precision
of needle-points, touch-downs on the moon.

I become the generation between and want
it both ways. I envy the pilots, so vigilant
and clean-shaven in their take-offs. Oh yes,
the civic, the impersonal, policy, loftiness.
I still need inheritances of clay and worms,
measured in roods, in feet and even thumbs.

Hands

Moments of illumination, spirals of days,
pigments, washes, the evening satchel
hung and the nights woken in a cell
by vellum worlds creaking in the breeze.
A voyage their image: longhanded cruises
over scraped and pumiced calf-skin,
the steer and yaw of these quill-driven
crossings as a reed trails its juices.
Anonymous seafarers. Whose were the hands?
A copyist loose-limbed, calm; another
sedate and careful. Or there's Brother
Extrovert's black and violet flamboyance.

Publishers of the word, desktop wedge
and stroke; their being a hand just
hinted in a margin. The face is lost,
a traveller congeals in traces of voyage.
Christ's tempter a scrawny Byzantine,
Hebrew names, those Asia Minor faces,
Matthew a posed Osiris, pillar-bases
of Viking brooches, that Coptic Virgin.
A nothingness of ego. The hand worships
by work. And it seems the rim becomes
a hub gathering spokes, the scriptorium's
stillness a geography at its fingertips.

The harbour is a scribe's last verse.
Two centuries since Columba had quilled
to a standstill. A serpent asks its coiled
question: Is patience a trust to rehearse

such detail? Sail on seven centuries
to Gutenberg's book. Think of a lifetime
inked in a concordance. Did they dream
warm presses, the software of memories?
Just look at Lot's wife! And how venial
her about-face there, arched and faded
under an *M*. Who watches too far ahead,
or behind? Tell us the voyage is all.

A Broken Line

She tenses at every bend so you almost feel
her will touching the brakepedal. Her body gears
into a curve as she turns a phantom steering wheel.

Dual control. It had to be like that for years.
Two children silhouetted on a yellow school-sign
flash past. 'Watch out in case...' – she dares.

A tart silence. So thinly she oversteps a line
between concern and meddling. *Now, mother what is it?*
Hurt, she vanishes in reverie: the silhouette on a sign

is a child standing at the school door, her favourite;
a desire to part with and hold still not reconciled,
hers and not hers, a contour in that morning light.

The moody years of being both adult and child.
Now so, so independent – CAUTION CONCEALED BENDS –
now, leaning on her shoulder weepy and spoiled.

A drowsiness is falling, falling. Miles of patience,
those roundabouts of tact, byroads of submission,
the long climbing hills. HARD SHOULDER ENDS.

The broken line runs on and on and on
centring a camber of road, langlauf of dashes,
Never-ending ski-strides of an abominable snowman.

She nods and jerks back to awareness. And yet
the road keeps gliding. She nods again. A whiplash
of vigilance. Down for the third time and out.

Sweet sleep of fecundity. The car speeds onwards.

Debonair

Against a tide of yawning suburbanites,
up the morning's street a homing débutante
links her dinner-jacketed cavalier, last night's
fling a carnation raffish in her ebony hair.

A down street commuter, out of the tail of my eye
I catch her recklessness, panache of such a beginning;
a rip-tide of energy, the home-goers pass by,
so debonair in that first circle of their laughter.

Feedback

Again this need to mend a world's mistakes.
For short-term gain,
Our fouled up shoreline, clogged lakes.
And sister earth is fretted: forest, air
A waterflow, a breeze, a rain,
Intricate fragile web and net. A young
Man rages 'Greed and waste
Unravel nests we share.'

I love that fledgling lavishness as he
Explains the scope and sweep
Of nature's sharing: even fungi
Can live absorbing algae cells' excess,
In turn defend a fellowship
Of lichen. Stubborn harmonies of growth.
The more I ripen, the more
I fathom youthfulness.

So strange how first ideals flame a mind,
The glare and flash of thought
Too sharp, too edged and undefined.
'Select your dreams,' I warn, 'they may come true.'
But do we round each other out?
My narrowed concentration steals his fire;
The blaze I'd focus warms
In me its breadth of view.

Voyage

Then finally land dropped out of sight
and we were completely at sea. I thought
of Meno's puzzle *How can we seek*
if we don't know where the harbour is?
But if we knew how could we've sought?
We left the deck in the falling light,

swayed to a table at a restaurant window.
French loaf and a carafe of Chianti.
We bend to talk and our heads arc
intimacy under the lampshade, a glow
small and warm against the immensity.
A bright corridor sails the dark.

Fragile as swallows beating the air,
two earthlings cross a narrow water
on a minor planet of an average star
turning somewhere in an outer region
among a hundred thousand million
galaxies. Shall one swallow fall?

The lamp counts the glints of your hair
as we savour a meal, each moment
its own reward, absolute fulfilment.
Far from soil, we dally over grain
and grape, fondling our bread and wine.

Middle of nowhere. Middle of everywhere.

Cosmos

'All right?' booms the saxophone man,
'everybody feeling chameleon?' The combo
expands the tune of a well-battered song.
An opulence of sound, clash and flow
as a spotlight tunnels dust in its beam,
glints the trumpet's bell and the hall
turns hot and hybrid, beery listeners
swaying and bobbing the mood of a theme.

From rainbows of timbre a strand of colour
floats into the air: the trumpet solo
burping one phrase of a melody, ripe
and brassy and buttoned down as though
a song is breathing over its origins,
those four hot-blooded notes weeping
their pleasure again on an old civil war
bugle. A sleazy backroom in New Orleans.

Sax and rhythm. The brightness of a reed,
winding tube and crook are working on
another hue of the tune that moves
into its own discourse: *Bud Freeman,*
Johnny Hodges, Charlie Parker. 'All right?'
he drawls, then scats a little as we clap
a tradition of subversions. But he's off again.
I watch swarms of dust in the spotlight,

swirls of galaxies, and imagine he's blowing
a huge balloon of space that's opening
our world of order. In a waft of creation
his being becomes a music's happening.
A red-shirted pianist now leans to seize
a gene of the song which seems to veer
and improvise, somehow catching a moment's
shifts and humours. Hail! Madam Jazz.

Let the theme return, its mutants echoing
as a tune balances against its freedom.
One key – so open-toned and open-stitched.

A beat poised, a crossgrained rhythm,
interplays, imbrications of voice over voice,
mutinies of living are rocking the steady
state of a theme; these riffs and overlappings
a love of deviance, our genesis in noise.

Is That?

Homing from a walk before turning in
we glance through someone's uncurtained window
lights and shades of another life. But
look! ours too are lit. It seems as though
we stand outside ourselves or shed a skin,
turning our world a moment inside out.

So, there it is: a room in the universe.
Somewhere on a map an arrow is pointing down:
you are here. A booth of translucence between
two gardens, a lampshade like a full moon.
Is that where we eat and talk and play, nurse
our abrasions, wonder how else it might have been?

Or where we shift and wake in sunny weather,
spoors of desire scattered across a floor,
a stocking wriggled like an eel, an out of fashion
tie my careless lasso, then nearer the door
shoes – tongued holsters, biographers in leather,
their furrowed intensities footnotes to a passion.

So many questions. A breath's silver fur
floats into an immensity of night. Too lost
in thought could a Cartesian ghost begin
to doubt his footfalls on a pavement frost?
Where's the key? Turn its smallness. Undoor
our swarms of dream, a world of outside in.

Welcome

In early spring talk still young and highflown
We laughed, there was an endless time to flirt
And toy with a fable of year. A snowdrop afloat
In an old wine glass on our table, already grown
Tumid with water, lifted the panels of her skirt
To show the pale green hem of her petticoat.

Soon we're strolling along the edge of a bay
Kicking over the traces of an early swimmer.
It's deep into June: summer lush and unplanned
Rocks us in its lazy arms. In the blaze of day
We paddle in the shallows, I watch in a shimmer
Of water the sun doodling honeycombs in sand.

A year tilts into autumn; after its madcap
Race our Russian vine issues its manifesto,
A spray of flower. The sun sloping in humility
Smiles its frail approval as old men wrap
Against the chill. At last I think I know
Half of what we love is love's fragility.

A winter evening as I turn into our street
I hurry to see the rim of light that fingers
Around the curtain's edge to tell you're home.
You open the door and I sense as we meet
Our moment's wonder. A scent lingers.
I breathe deeply to feed memory's honeycomb.

Rhapsody

1. *Mid-points*

Nothing will stay still. You stretch to touch
but cannot catch, just graze it as it slips
out of reach. Yet savour it now its passing,
at once an aftertaste that shakes the buds

of memory and foretaste of eternities to come.
Look, there is the marvel! But as you look,
You look behind, beside, between, beyond.
The lush sumac hides crimson and banana
hues, fragrances remind both of bygones
and tomorrow in the crow's foot and furrow
dimpled children smile, genes bloom
eons glide between your butter-fingers.
Have you so outgrown the age of time?
Prod of insight or knock on sanity's wall?
Scorch of wisdom's love or lure of madness?
A little quietude you ask, yet not
the balance that finds a point of equilibrium.
Rather choose the tense delight that knows
tug of was, pull of will-be, that is
the calm of motion you desire. Always
all hovers in its changing, every instant's
gene pivots possibilities, mid-points,
diminished chords poised between tonalities.
You strike the moment's note, then overtone
over overtone ascends in fractions to where
all honest notes gather and are one.

2. *Flow*

This love that is forever is in motion,
a coiling stream of now and now and now.
Remember, remember a wistful time,
sunlit age, upstream once and long ago,
a paradise of past when all is well –
how things have changed! Or tomorrow you say,
tomorrow, maybe downstream soon and hilly
in the green far-away, if only when,
if only then you say – but it is now
a world of happening forever is in motion,
now and here nothing will stand still,
our point of departure the actual; though
we search for footholds in what was or will be
or with a god's eye view attempt detachment
to minimise our risks, human and fallible we
trust the love that is surrender to the flow.

In all this flux perhaps some patterns form:
eddies, rondos of experience, spirals, spheres
of remembrance, loops of history, forecast or guess;
yet you are never there, never have arrived,
for there is no *status quo*, moment by moment
like planets tense within our orbits, we trust,
we choose, we act and so become our story,
we do and tell our own once-upon-a-time.
Still there is room for surprise: we live
at the mercy of each new event, beck
and call of mystery, vulnerable to how it is.
Speak of glancing water or ever-fresh
configurations of a sky; flowing and mutable,
this love that is forever is in motion
and every here and now a widening ring.

Between

As we fall into step I ask a penny for your thoughts.
'Oh, nothing,' you say, 'well, nothing so easily bought.'

Sliding into the rhythm of your silence, I almost forget
how lonely I'd been until that autumn morning we met.

At bedtime up along my childhood's stairway, tongues
of fire cast shadows. Too earnest, too highstrung.

My desire is endless: others ended when I'd only started.
Then, there was you: so whole-hog, so wholehearted.

Think of the thousands of nights and the shadows fought.
And the mornings of light. I try to read your thought.

In the strange openness of your face, I'm powerless.
Always this love. Always this infinity between us.

Summerfest

1. *Open Air*

A first balmy evening and we've got together.
Chatter and music of a party seem to overflow
As we spill out into a sudden gift of weather,
Gathering around tables on a hot-bricked patio.
Even the solstice days were wet and overcast,
It was easy to lose faith when July fell away.
A season has held fire, kept best until last,
This must surely be the decade's hottest day.
The hostess is everywhere topping up glasses.
Miraculous as Cana's water, a courtesy and ease
Spreads among her chosen guests. She passes
By, her trace a slight hint of a warm breeze.
An August evening breathes its final sunshine;
This night will turn our summer back to wine.

2. *Shadows*

Dark. The hostess leans over our table to alter
The wick in a small coloured lantern she's lighting,
Her back sunned between the bows of a silk halter,
The curve of her shoulder blade a folded wing.
A mood seems to blur our lines of joy and sorrow
In warm flutters of a candle, a wine-glass blushes.
Whose gentle shadows roam this garden we borrow,
Whose children once played among these bushes?
Through an open window a saxophone climbs a loud
Sad tune, pouring its soul and still unable
To tell why the fall of one late summer's night
Falters a moment over the loneness in a crowd.
An angel of memory has hovered near our table;
So many shades have loved this garden's sunlight.

3. *Sway*

The dance! the dance! everybody on their feet!
Move wine-loosened, quick-footed, rhythm-driven
And turn wild variations on what we're given;
Tilt and wheel, throb of the nodded upbeat.
Already we've become the dance; bodies and minds
A sweated ecstasy, a pulsing frenzy of control;
Our faces, vague and happy, merge into a whole
Delirium of summer. All that was wound unwinds.
A oneness of weaving and bobbing in the night air;
Again and again this play of check and freedom,
A jazz pulling against the sameness of the drum,
Our motion fallen in love with going nowhere.
Swirl, let-go, comeback. A flirtatious liaison.
Some dream in the dance's sway goes on and on.

A Fragile City

(1 9 9 5)

Ὁ κόσμος οὗτος μία πόλις ἐστί

This world of ours is one city.

EPICTETUS

FILTERED LIGHT

Euch kommt jeden Morgen das neue Licht
warm in die offene Wohnung.
Und ihr habt ein Gefühl von Gesicht zu Gesicht,
und das verleitet zur Schonung.

Every morning new light comes
warmly into the open house
and you have a feeling that moves from face to face
and that leads you astray to caring.

RAINER MARIA RILKE
translated by Robert Bly

Transit

Urgencies of language: check-in, stand-by, take-off.
Everything apace, businesslike. But I'm happy here
Gazing at all the meetings and farewells. I love
To see those strangers' faces quickened and bare.
A lost arrival is wandering. A moment on edge,
He pans a lounge for his countersign of welcome.
A flash of greeting, sudden lightening of baggage,
As though he journeyed out only to journey home.
I watch a parting couple in their embrace and freeing.
The woman turns, a Veronica with her handkerchief
Absorbing into herself a last stain of a countenance.
She dissolves in crowds. An aura of her leaving glance
Travels through the yearning air. Tell me we live
For those faces wiped into the folds of our being.

Folding

Our summer hide-out was the crotch of an old sumac,
A bole V-ing upwards into its light and pliancy,
Our feet in the fork, its boughs against our back;
A huddle of inclusiveness, first inkling of diversity.
Who was that strange child, that face at the rim
Demanding vision? It's as if our tree contracted,
Refusing the danger of renewal. A closing system.
That face returns and returns where never expected:
The Jewish woman in Chicago whose stare was rife
With memory or that Aran widower unfurling his story.
We seem to fold into each other, upsurges of a life
Drawing me into a seamless time, their past
A vibrancy of absence leaving its traces in me.
Is the child at the rim every stranger I've faced?

Beyond

Ask me then and I'm almost sure I'd say
A hand, a turn of shoulder, some voluptuous
Bend of playfulness kept inviting my caress.
Those days I talked of *truth* and *beauty*.
It was your expression. Those eyes that welcomed
Without reserve. Open-faced, so much a brother's
Keeper. It's as though we surrendered each other's
Freedom, freeing the other the more we succumbed.
It was years later I thought of Dante's Beatrice,
And how once you'd chided me for making fun
Of an old man. *Who knows what he's undergone?*
A face is filtering light from beyond a face.
You'd seen transparence in a stranger's infinite
Gaze. I moved in your light to see the light.

News

It was a struggle, but he arrived just after one.
Daniel George his father names him by telephone.
An unbroken line. And so he enters our universe
God's my judge, Soil-worker as his grandfathers.
Who's he like? I try to imagine his countenance
A little smudged, but finding its own structure
From genes and traces, incessant recommencements
Travelling towards a future. A recourse and rupture.
It's as though two separatenesses had come together
Blending their need with desire, a self and other,
Some kind of surplus in a lovers' touch and go.
Daniel George. One face of renewal and overflow.
Yours and not yours. You are and are not your son.
Fecundity's old riddle and a world moving on.

Quartet

These players nod and gleam as if they're seeing
And hearing the other's expression, each leaning
Into the fine-nerved strings, their whole being
Vested in this interplay, this gamble on meaning.
I remember a crescendo dream. We burned and burned.
Maybe it's age. I grow in this mutual succumbing:
Bow and pluck, phrase and breath of an earned
And watchful passion, our face to face becoming.
All shall be equal we'd said. But nothing matches.
Overlaps. Voice-overs. A sudden fertile digression
Loops into our rousing silence. Something over-reaches
Equality, a lived-in music shaping my compassion.
The conversation dips and wanders and tenses again.
A shining between faces, a listening inward and open.

Flare

There we were a cluster of twenty-year-olds.
A colour, a timbre fixes the sweep of that mood:
Cheap Chianti, candlelight, damp sugar-bowls,
A readiness to change a world half-understood.
No, nothing could ever again be the same.
Raise a mug of wine, a hymn to the proletariat.
The system's so damned unfair. But we had a dream.
We shall overcome. We'll sing our hearts out.
That chorus and I recall how our faces would blur
Into sameness. *Deep in my heart I still believe.*
Was it a cry for meaning we'd begun to squander,
Our well-meant vision turned faceless and assertive?
An energy flickers the untrimmed wick of a dream.
Our innocent anger keeps scattering the flame.

Focus

Our hurried need to flare and blaze both ends.
How slowly we'd grow, option by tiny option.
Catch us again, now that a fifth decade bends
Our lived-in dream, a jet of steadied vision.
Maybe I've learned to fear the sweeping chorus:
The masses, the system. Something cuts deeper.
Remember how young compassion first moved us:
A solo beseeching face calling me its keeper?
I reach across those years to re-focus a dream
Throwing its light again as our chorus fades;
My cupped hands sheltering the glow of a flame,
I see now in those eyes where their story leads.
Each life is thickening into its own fabric.
Every face so utterly itself. Alone. Unique.

Tension

The wrong voice, self-righteous, somehow out of tune:
Mr Chairman, I object to my colleague's actions.
One by one around the table we cast our stone.
He put a good face on it. Then, I saw he winced.
But where have I seen those hunted eyes before?
Frenchie, let's get Frenchie! The victim's glance
As he bolted hell for leather up a school corridor;
The patent shoes and corduroys, a swarthy difference.
I know the rules, but I want to halt this sacrifice.
My neighbour whispers: 'he's got to be taken to task,
A question of solidarity'. Does a fish squirm in a net?
I'm full of qualms. Was it just the tone of voice?
A face forgets a face breathing behind a mask.
The heart and the mind. Tensing poles of a magnet.

Casualty

She's at it again. Of course, she'll never learn.
Once she touches the stuff – well, that's that.
I read about it and know this classic pattern:
No insight and rock-bottom always too late.
We go on and on talking. All those far-fetched
Excuses, this ravelling of schemes and make-believe.
Am I the theory-man, trying to keep us detached?
History judges history and here's a write-off.
But her mother and sister are up again tonight.
The pancreas. Someone must drive her to casualty.
And besides there's the child; such a fright
Could bring his asthma on. In their fuss and care
I turn towards a countenance so alone and singular.
Something in her tragedy faces and outfaces me.

Revelation

Our train gains ground into the evening light.
Among the trees the sun catches in its fall
Glints and anglings of a stone in a distant gable,
A broadcast of facets, one and infinite.
I glance at you. There's so much unexplained.
Plays of your light keep provoking my infinity;
Already something in your presence overflows me,
A gleam of a face refusing to be contained.
How little I know of you. Again and again
I've resolved to be the giver and not the taker,
Somehow to surpass myself. Am I the mapmaker
So soon astray in this unknowable terrain?
Twenty-one years. And I'm journeying to discover
Only what your face reveals. Stranger and lover.

Translation

The tiler was deaf and dumb. He charmed all
With blue-eyed nods and signs until we forgot
His blemish. He pencilled needs on a bare wall:
2 ornamentals, 7 borders, ¹/₂ tub of grout.
One morning, his thumb and index shape a ring,
As he motions me aside to show a snapshot.
His face glows in this lover's mute naming
But a forefinger signals 'I'm slitting my throat'.
I smile at shyness, a sudden boyish withdrawal.
Is freedom our knowing that freedom is at stake?
He's young and hot in his leather. So I translate
Across trusting years into our male tick-tack.
My palms curve in the air a female figure 8.
I blow from my fingertips a kiss of approval.

Light

She tires easily, I'm warned, just a short while.
Well past ninety, a voyage fulfilled and intense.
I bend to kiss her. She smiles her girl's smile,
A presence begun absenting itself from a presence.
Surely she must be aware she's about to depart.
A strange translucence, an expression almost younger
And keener, as if she's taking the world to heart.
A boundless desire, a hunger nourished by hunger.
She has heard on the news of a newly discovered star,
A billion years it must journey our empty spaces;
The immensity of a conversation's flow and counterflow
Commands me with eyes I seem to answer to and for.
Beauty is truth, truth beauty. That is all ye know...
What is this light that falls between two faces?

Aversion

In fair Verona where we lay our scene. The theatre's
Warm as a festering London. Juliet and her banished
Romeo dally in the orchard, menders of their begetters'
Grudges. *Some shall be pardon'd and some punished.*
Another plot vibrates in me. A Norwegian ('The Slut'
She's called) flees with a German soldier, chooses
Her sweet, neutral days cooped in a Swedish hut.
They're found and shot. *A plague on both your houses.*
Cleansed and resolved, I exit headily to the street.
Of all people, look who's approaching! – a colleague
Who'd always done me down. I want our gaze to meet,
A single gesture. Enough dissembling and intrigue.
A glance averted and we've passed each other by.
Our long fallen history, one twinkling of an eye.

VEILS AND MASKS

Bortom era ord anade jag era ansikten.
De ansikten ni bär är inte era verkliga.
Ni var förklädda maskerade beslöjade.
Era obeslöjade ansikten är vakrare...

Beyond your words I sensed your faces.
The faces you bear are not your real ones.
You were disguised masked veiled.
Your unveiled faces are more beautiful...

MIRJAM TUOMINEN
translated by David McDuff

Intrusion

The glaze of loved and lover,
our amorous self-containment,
concentric and utterly present
to the other. Sweetest hour.

But what if between our gazes
shadows of the stricken fall,
the stares we seem to veil
keep on commanding us?

Our two-ness is never alone.
Whose is that intrusive face
that looms unseen between us
condemning all we haven't done?

The eclipsed. The destitute.
O sly worm of dominance
coiling its own discountenance,
our masks and blottings out.

Is love a threadbare blindfold?
'Yes,' say our shadows, 'unless
you turn to face the faceless.'
Who'll re-envisage the world?

How?

When the time comes, how will we have been:
giver or hoarder, sharers or sleek *gringos?*
Children of the barrio, how can I explain?

Silk I love: fall and flow and cocoon,
the worm's sheen, desire clinging and loose.
When the time comes, how will we have been?

And fruits: plums, tangerines, seedy moon
of a kiwi, yellow-orange flesh of mangos,
children of the barrio, how can I explain?

Or cheeses skinned with peppers, a stilton
waxy, wrinkle-rinded, my blue-veined gorgonzolas.
When the time comes, how will we have been?

Morning curtains, towels lilac and green
in the light, the pile of a rug scuffing toes,
children of the barrio, how can I explain?

Something cries its grievance. A false coin
is spinning: heads I win, tails you lose.
When the time comes, how will we have been?
Children of the barrio, how can I explain?

Outsider

A sheltered arch or where underground
kitchens of an inn sent
through grids of pavement grating
the warmth of the ass's breath –
Where did last night's Christ lie down?

Every morning for months I watched
a man I might have been,
about my age and bearded too,
his face blotched crimson
with cheap wine and sleeping rough.

He walked the far side of the street
always hurrying somewhere;
a father who couldn't praise, I wondered,
or what had blurred his star?
For months our eyes never met,

though the street between us was narrow,
until that eve he crossed.
'Some help,' he said, but it must have been
my double's eyes that asked
where would He lie down tomorrow?

An old outsider within me winced,
shook him off and fled;
that street between was so narrow –
I chose the inn and was afraid.
I'm sure I've never seen him since –

but tomorrow when carafes go round
a lone presence will pass
tremors through our frail togetherness;
again those eyes will ask
where did last night's Christ lie down?

Tables

1

'You know yourself, nothing but money counts.'
I try my best to smile my knowing smile.
Nods to an age's spirit, a self-effacement.

So often he's the enabler, a hidden hand lent.
'On bread alone?' But any doubt is scandal.
I swallow mutinous words as the tables turn.

What did I ever know of deprivation? His scorn
whips me: shame, insecurity, angst that haunts
a body all its life. Nothing. I know nothing.

Self-made, yet so many taken under his wing.
Even innocence must sometimes wear a mask.
'That's talk for ascetics or the too well-off!'

2

An ascetic? No. A mortal who loves to eat
sharon fruits, blancmange, to sip iced rosé
or feel warm sand on the arches of his feet.

Young Keats dressed and quiffed for his table.
I bath early, grooming and scenting myself;
silked and rakish, I'm ready to love invisible

muses. Then everything cloys except the journey.
Endless desert. I feed on some hump of memory
and expectation. Ecstasy moving and stationary,

a delight fuelling itself. Unlimited supply
and demand. The end of desire is more desire.
My camel soul must travel the needle's eye.

3

He's sleeping rough. There but for a woman's praise
assuaging my temperament. (Who'll shelter my double?)
I tuck my knee-caps into the hollows of her knees.

And still he haunts me, my vagabond counterpart.
I know Thomas More brought beggars to his table.
Every loop of the mind I try keeps falling short.

So much dereliction I know I can't countenance.
Justice is a faceless scales. Tell me who'll be
the rich man sighting that prodigal in the distance

to fall on his neck and kiss him? The love cup
raised in celebration of a father's huge abandon;
the art of giving, the art of never giving up.

Hostel

Station of ease for the broken or frail.
A tear in an ocean. And yet that welcome
At face value, a roof and warmth, a meal.
Vague signals of angeldom.

So little. So short of grand revolution
We'll always want to dream of.
If only dreams could scoop or fill an ocean...
Thimbled gestures of a love,

Some gift of falling for endless tasks
Berth this moment's care;
The scarred visage of a down-and-out who asks
If an ocean starts with a tear?

Patient logs of strays and have-nots.
A youth stubborn and hurt
Uproots and wanders. No one knows his whereabouts,
Nomad and introvert.

Long headstrong years on the loose;
Now shattered and underfed
A quarrelsome body yields nightly to delicious
Mercies of bath and bed.

One evening and again he's gone
Without trace. No mendings. No rebirth.
Tiny alleviations, something beautiful done.
A caress on the face of the earth.

Theft

Another wired photograph of an African woman
Holding a small girl with a pear-shaped head
And a shrivelled crowfooted face. Has someone
Thieved a child, left her this elf instead?

Drought. Failed crops. And the rains too late.
Hollows of famine rumble the bowels of the earth.
Look long and deep. Unable to clean forget,
I begin my day, busy in the lap of the north.

Little knoweth the fat what the lean doth mean.
I can't ghost-write a suffering. Only my guess
And leap, flickers of memory or the unforeseen.
I know how easily a world unsheathes my tinyness.

But nothing appeases her stare. Again I'll pore
Over this image of hunger. Is compassion a guilty
Fear of *there but for fortune* or is there more?
It's as though something in her gaze commands me.

A look both rapt and implacable. There's no wool
To pull over these eyes. Look long. Look deeper.
Cycles of dominance; a hemisphere's rise and fall.
She stares and stares. Am I my sister's keeper?

Two After Dark

1

I tuned in that night to a man's ageing voice:
'I'm fancy-free. I could have had my pick of them.'
An eavesdropper, had I already begun to pity him?

'Maybe if you're tethered young, you get used to it.
All you needed was the gab and a good way with you.
On the dance-floor I was as smart as any on my feet.

'Out there with a steady, if I saw a handsomer woman
I'd watch my chance. *But haven't you a girl with you?*
It's you I want, I'd say, *and sure don't mind anyone.*'

I stare at a wireless trying to envisage his face.
'And I did a great trade in women from far and near.'
An old notched gun smoking stubbornly in the corner.

2

I remembered sitting in half-light with an old friend
Stitching years we'd missed. But as night came on
I knew I'd heard her hearing my unasked question.

'I waited,' she laughed, 'for a prince to come riding
On a white horse.' Always one of us, she'd refused
To flatter or fawn; confidante and equal in everything.

A nature that had to give all. Why anything less?
She used to say 'Wait till I'm minister for fairness!'
Just wait. That was a time when we owned the world.

Men. Where will they all fade with their giddiness?
No prince. She rose, making her way across the dark
To a lamp, luminous and surefooted in her apartness.

Rowing Back

If she broached him near the bone, like his father
He'd abscond, then, reappear in his boat to pout
For hours on end in the bay, sitting it out
Till she came beckoning guiltily from the shore.

I see him there shame-faced, glad of a let-out,
As hunching on his oars he turned and back-tracked,
Sullen but somehow holding his maleness intact,
Frail dignity balanced on the keel of a boat.

Come clean. What is it we've been so afraid of?
A fear of what we couldn't tame, wild otherness
Wobbling and ungraspable, a sway and completeness.
We row an unfathomable sea. Comber and trough.

Tumble and come-back. A filling tide's action
And passivity, slow logic of retreats and charges,
As wave into wave keeps gaining on itself, surges
Beyond our control and so full of direction.

But something in her expression is veiled and denied.
Those old patterns of huff, guilt and climb-down.
The ghosts of so many women are standing alone
Waving to an oarsman brooding on his phantom pride.

Is the boat in the bay cradling a dread of failure,
A bravado trying to face up to its loss of face?
Visible and invisible as children cribbing disgrace
Behind our fingers, forgive us as we row ashore.

At the Hairdresser's

My neck on the porcelain rim, a tautness unbends
Backwards into suds and rushes and squirts of water.
A teenage girl (she could easily be my daughter)
Gentles my head. Surely a world is safe in her hands?
Through the steamy towels and scissorings a radio
Blurts news from the East. Some million men dug in.
Our sly litany, old stealthy dream of domination:
Silkworm, jaguar, tomcat, hawkeye, sea-sparrow.
Her thumbs spiral deep into a skull of memory.
Sully's and Quinner's gangs fight for a school fort
With hedge-cuttings bound into whips. Lash and hurt
And threat of 'sissy' or 'coward'. Above all, don't cry.
My clogged maleness loosens in her determined fingers.
Those helmeted faces so boyish with their unspilt tears.

Embrace

The evening guests arrive, all flowers and wine
and loud hellos at the gate. *Come on, come in.*
Good to see you! Just a bottle for the kitchen.
I kiss the women's cheeks; between us, the men,
a handshake, our gesture and show of strength,
this double signal – hands-on and armslength.

I want to fling my limbs open and embrace.
A clumsy left hand glances a shoulder blade
and I know at once he's feeling some hand laid
to measure a deal's anxiety, nervous give-aways.
A hug is a dagger too close, a dealer's grope.
Something tightens at my touch and buttons up.

I'll take your coat. Flowers. You shouldn't have!
We shy from such receiving, a chink in the male
like a sideways revelation and a hurried withdrawal
or some blurted late-night confidence brushed off
in a morning-after silence or averted look.
Was I bad? I remembered nothing when I woke.

What have we done to ourselves? Years of tautness,
a gaucheness hiding its face behind our ritual,
a coil and wriggle in ourselves we want to veil.
Look! how those women caress and touch with ease.
Sisters, sisters, it's us you're trying to free;
more than your scorn, our dealer's grope needs pity.

And weren't you women once those mothers drying
up our tears? A face shown and withdrawn.
Slugs and snails and puppy dogs. *Stand like a man.*
Tell me, did you ever see your father crying?
A coin's faces, each a keeper for the other.
Woman and man, somehow we're in this together.

Tracks

1

How it sways in its tracks as it gathers speed!
We steady ourselves against any lurch of intimacy,
our deflected faces guarding invisible territory.

The jolted halt, the scurried terrazzo passage,
as elbow to elbow we show our tickets and wedge
towards morning. So much changed and unchanged.

Thousands of years, of mornings, of jostling men:
hunters, tool-users, ranchers, traders, explorers.
Defining. Redefining. Makers and crossers of borders.

Thousands of years, of mornings, of nourishing women,
protectors of inlands, rearers, nurturers, faithful
guardians of hearth, keepers of hive and churn.

We're shoulder to shoulder in this rush and scrum
of a morning. Subtler and more persistent, you wear
our masks and will outwit us. But was there a dream?

The train moves on, grumbling in the frame of a bridge
like a man moaning the linear premise of his station,
a zigzag of life swerving on its narrow gauge.

Our crush on living daylight tapers forwards.
When will you come bringing the milk and honey,
spilling a heartland over our rigid borders?

2

I'd waited all afternoon for her to return.
I glanced through a window at an empty road
of nunnish spruces, tall and dark and stern,
watching over asphalt where it had snowed
on and off, a vague but persistent caress
of muslin laid across a road's aloneness.

Hours delayed, she came laden with apologies:
a colleague ill – someone had to cover for him,
a report due tomorrow; then, halfway home,
the return to check in case pipes would freeze.

Her giving is so easily absorbed. A thermostat
of concern smoothes the air. Earth mother. Fail-safe.
Heavy-footed angel I tread in with talk of
'staking out territory' and 'leaving it at that'.

Am I my mask? Our one-track compulsion to define
as a lavishness strives to expand our given space.
A sudden mantilla of doubt is shadowing her gaze:
'Why aren't we women as good at drawing the line?'

For a while, side by side, in the dusk we stood
and watched another shower, inhaling the slow
pervasion of a fall seizing on nothing, a mood
of persistence and letting be, its touch-and-go
decking spruces like brides, a mousse of zigzags
blurring and undoing the car's determined tracks.

La Différence

1 *Clash*

Suddenly you shrink – a carapace of pain.
Outsider I blunder further into protest.
Why? For heaven's sake try to explain.

Another wound. Hurt of a hurt unnoticed.
Can a man learn nothing but words? I bluster
clumsy half-sentences; thick-skinned, ham-fisted.

'If only you'd told me.' Instead you fester,
harbour a wordlessness that keeps trying to say
'to have to say is to fail'. My best filibuster

empties into silence. A mood leaves its highway
of huff-no-move stumbling towards self-reproach.
Am I the oafish male? And so we parley:

'If I were you I'd feel the same,' I approach
a sideways acknowledgement, a first breakthrough.
Words match words, the love-straws we clutch.

More the tomboy, more the sissy; atonement of two.
Dice of genes and *vive la différence*.
Woman me as I am manning you.

2 *Neighbour*

Me – possess you? See how I look
into your eye, human and similar.
I face a neighbour's face and talk
the common sense of common gender.

Much more the same than different:
fears, countless yearnings, our gauze
of meanings. So, by one consent
the welcome and appeal of face to face.

A delicate line of balance. But then
the rounds of your eyes grow murky,
the dark tips of your lashes lengthen,
a tremble in your aura caresses me.

Me – know you? So utterly more
different than the same. A modesty
absent in its presence, glory of desire;
something revealed, then drawn away.

3 *Nurses*

Staunch and calm in the dimmed light –
a charted pulse, a careful tuck –
I heed the dark sway of their bodies
as they keep watch, their rockabye
voices mothering towards sleep.

Where am I? Awareness sneaks
again to notice flushes of light,
lemon streaks of dawn re-establish
window-panes. I must have fallen off,
let ages slip through the sashes?

Allegro, full of good mornings
and how are we today Mr O'?
Girls with slender arms tidy
pillows, bring bowls of water
to swab and towel and daughter me.

Such young strides, such narrow waists!
They smile and know: born of women,
always theirs, they know beyond
my knowing. I yearn in their secret,
I sleep and wake in their wonder.

In the End

So I've confessed the cargo of my gender;
I know the subtle ways we've faced you down.
Maybe I've been more fortunate than others?

In the end I can only speak from experience.
I delight in womanhood. A marvel infinitely
refined. Nuances of strength. Their presence.

Together in everything, what veil of mystery
still falls between us? All I can't seize
seems to possess me. Comrade and mistress.

I love those tiny derailments of control
inviting me into the magnanimity of woman.
Unvisored. Somehow loosened in my role,

I wear a different mask, living and porous,
a delicious obedience to all my voices
allowing our musics their pitch and part.

Your freedom is our freedom. And I relearn
a forgotten register. Inward and airborne,
a soprano is gliding in my womanish heart.

Wisconsin

In May the Menomonie fishers show by the Lake
to spear some last treaty right in the shallows;
the local boys ride the water, jeer and smack
the waves, bucking their speedboat bronchos.

Someone, for God's sake, stop those bastards! Again
the absolute rage of youth: send back Mayflowers,
missioners with beads and guns, the frontiersmen,
caravels with their bellies full of conquistadores.

Our old indulgent dream of untouched races,
peace-pipe smokers, growers of squash and maize.
But they had drifted southward, married fur traders
and changed. Into the shifting muddle of what is

my anger blends. It's all too stitched in time,
the seams, the folds, the overlaps and patches.
Do you hear those outboard engines' scream?
We belong, we belong. Stop stabbing our conscience!

I think of Las Casas picking up the pieces
as regimes fall and one plan after another
sunders. He begins all over again; a business
unfinished, a ghost possessed by the word brother.

Doorway

I'd climbed the engineer's cabin steps, knocked
Like a schoolboy: Could I have a word with you?
There he stands in flannels, his navy blue
Blazer shining, framed by a door he's blocked.

'I'll give a man a hearing,' he says. I back
Downwards a little, still trying to glimpse
His face. It's London nineteen sixty-six.
Whoever he thinks he sees is probably black

Or at best a step beneath. And I'm effaced.
I stand under sentence: guilt by motherland,
Overseen by some blindness I won't understand.
A degradation: such pride and so much waste.

But I grow older, begin to wonder if he
Like Plato's tyrant stared at empty space,
Confronting nothing and I was a shadow whose face
Had long turned away. I refuse this history.

I'm still climbing to a door, trying to retrace
Those steps. Tell me why you're afraid of me?
How lonely the eye in its majesty. See me.
Hold my gaze. I'm nothing but this naked face.

Shame

A mind already smitten;
rife and cloven cells,
alien vessels
of scorn doubling within.

In Pimlico Araners who shrank
when someone had spoken Irish,
a brand and blemish.
What would the Blacks think?

That African minister's rage;
his state-car blocked by a herdsman's
flock, he threatens
and shouts *Sauvage! Sauvage!*

Bitter moment of corrosion
when all that might have praised
turn to dust.
Iron eats into iron.

Progress

1

News of a truce broken. More shootings.
Young insurgents with sights fixed on square
one, some golden age about to rebegin.
A sweeping clean.
Always a flow in the flow of things,
will we ever start where we are?

Remember whose youth once fell for
loserdom, cragged faces of island people,
dream moment of a life standing still.
A glorious idol.
Or when it changed, how I'd begin to abhor
their cussedness, muddled and untameable.

Strange irony. Hairpin bend of fate.
The heart spawns our reason's overreach,
faces that moved us blur behind a veil
of pure ideal:
age-old lure of the clean slate,
of worlds begun from scratch.

2

The Suquamish kissing our earth as sister,
Antarchos the Greek centring the sun,
our Christ-Jew bannering the conquistador:
so much ravelled and then undone.

So many wisdoms won and suppressed
or the bitter foolishness of wisdom marred;
as if ground once gained is more than lost
and we keep returning in order to depart.

Something must love our rise, our lapses:
the contingent, the unforeseen, the fluent;
sideways and scrambled our tumbling process,
made or broken in the fullness of a moment.

Abel

I seem to follow the lure and flow of a story.
Then glimpses of a garden or a school dormitory
Shift and interchange. The frames begin to slip
Quicker than I understand. I'm losing my grip.
Why this crowd? And why are they hunting me?
Faster and faster. Suddenly I'm on a promontory,
The frenzy of chase closing its faceless threat.
Over the edge. I've woken in a snow of sweat.

Frenchie, let's get Frenchie. Again a tableau
Of schoolboy persecution sways in some undertow
Of memory. I hear the swishing wavelike noise
Of a mob in hot pursuit. Our ritual sacrifice.
A sallow and dapper stranger weaves and dodges
Down a corridor with a swarm of blurred visages
Close on his heels, whipping boy and scapegoat,
A swoon of oneness singling his difference out.

This evening in a country that I'd first come
To half a life ago, some blond youths loom
Up the platform, beer-cans glinting in the dark.
My suspicious swarthness. A Greek or even a Turk?
'Is it here we trounce foreigners?' sneers a voice,
Partly his show for the gang, partly his menace.
An ugly moment. I hurry on trying to pretend
I didn't understand, scanning exits for my friend.

Unbroken line of pogroms, this blindman's buff.
A planet now at stake, perhaps we know enough
To reveal even the slants and bias of our lens?
A stark figure transverses our shed millennia,
That first victim forever crying his innocence.
Stay the knife. Children of a jealous violence,
Fugitives on the earth, may we still ask his pardon?
Say to me, brother Abel, that I'm your guardian.

BOUNDARIES

Springbrunn är du, vars soligt glittrande stråle
skön i sin jämvikt, skön i sin formstränga båge,
skön i sin styrka, äger
makten att älska gränser och ädla mått.

A fountain you are, whose sunnily glittering beam,
beautiful in its equilibrium, beautiful in its form-strict arc,
beautiful in its strength, possesses
the power to love limits and noble dimensions.

KARIN BOYE
translated by David McDuff

Hopscotch

Our chalked figure of boxes squared
off and interlocked. Overlappings
of sides, t-shapes, half-shared
divides. A groundwork for high jinks.

'Your go!' And everyone hunkers to watch
if I toe the line. Footfall vigil.
Is this why the Germans call hopscotch
'playing a game of heaven and hell'?

Such passion for limits and thresholds.
Johnston's shop in Pettigo, its entrances
in both counties. A foot in two worlds.
Abutment and frontier. Old ambivalences.

Or the way sometimes exact same sounds
seemed to slide and play with words;
a child is riddling out how 'bounds'
means 'confines' and 'bounces forwards'.

Then, the pivot homewards. Our swift
about-face. Thrill and crisis of turning;
one ankle clasped, one hand aloft,
frail balance of gravity and yearning.

A skittish jump. Again our spreadeagle
heavy-footed landings astride a border.
Stop-go momentum of hop and straddle.
That need of lines. That leap's desire.

Noon

I've fallen in love again with gazing.
A lake is absorbing shimmered transfers
of grey alders and ripplings of leaves.

A hollow twig hesitates, then steers
outward, canoeing this ice-age maw.
Mountain eye. Basin of contemplation.

A skimmed stone tumbles and disappears.
Minutiae of an aeon. Noon is filling
the air with its riddles. Who am I?

Archaeologies of thought define me:
the words I use, phrases, gestures.
Is everything seen with an encoded eye?

Piecemeal layers of address and response.
Process of encounters: fall-out, settlings,
accruals, a womb of residues and ores.

Silent undertows. Still-living sediment.
A mountain lake swallows and endures
these slow, deep accumulations of sludge.

In the dark and light of every about-face
some beckoning aim, a hovering remembrance.
My spirit is watching over the waters.

Story

A man turns hostage for his friend's release:
It is a far, far better rest that I go to...
Abandon without return. Gratuity of sacrifice.

It is a far, far better thing that I do...
that cadenza of Dickens's *Tale of Two Cities*
and a child bursts in tears. Must it be so?

One story will haunt him all his living days.
The wartime girl with her German soldier flees
over the frontiers. Or tell him, now as he greys,

of an African spirit between one world and another
who stays around as a child just to make happy
the bruised face of a woman who'd become his mother.

My name is made illustrious in the light of his.
To break and enter another's brokenness and glory.

This is the story I'll touch in every caress.

Sunlight

Two children swimming out to the low tide rocks
and a woman watching. Breaststrokes. Headlong
aspirations of dips and bobs across the water.

Her lovely givenness a vigilance of substitution,
hostage to every breath and splash. Stange paradox:
the further they swim away, the nearer they are.

*'That's my place in the sun' is how the usurpation
of the whole world began.* And I fill with wonder
watching a woman watching. What is this reflex?

An abandon and weightlessness of concern. Pure
undergoing. Almost as if they float in the matrix
of her being, drifting in passivities of creation.

Some overflow of boundaries weaves its intrigues
of motherhood. A debt being payed before the loan,
as though she usurps herself in watching over

the whirl of their busy limbs oaring back water
in sunlight, the whole gown of her life turned
inside out. Her face glories in this reversal.

Some obsessive patience hears an ungiven order.
Does an echo somehow anticipate its sound?
She's so full of answers before they ever call.

Merging

Nursing your cold's fever I'm forever nine
Worrying by my mother's bedside years ago.

A blind is drawn low to guard her eyes from sunshine,
Slowly I wipe her brow with a sponge. It's as though

Two women are merging into one. I swab her hairline,
Breathing and undergoing all she'll have to undergo.

A sudden exhaustion seizes me. Now I watch for a sign.
Maybe she's begun to doze. I leave. Sneaking. Tiptoe.

I wanted to be the Samaritan pouring my oils and wine.
But was I some skulking Levite abandoning her pillow?

I know to serve you better I need to hold the line,
Yet where that line should go, how can I ever know?

Here nursing your fever will I be forever nine?
You gaze a gaze that seems to say: 'To think it's so,

To think for someone else even this face of mine
Is the face of a certain man going down to Jericho.'

Dusk

Look! a pair courting against the mauve
Of evening. Silhouettes caress on a bandstand,
Fold in their oneness. (Was it so long ago?)
We draw close and pass their no-man's-land
The first oblivion of kisses *quid pro quo*,
Those sweet trade-offs of *prima facie* love.

I glance their desire. Again a riddling elf
Of wisdom dances: are we only found in loss?
In going beyond our frontiers do we return?
Without reserve. Chosen even before I choose.
A first dalliance throws its nets of concern.
Matrices of care. Strange ecologies of self.

On a bench in fallen light that elderly couple
Tilt their bodies in a long mutual attention
Of nods and silence. Gestures seem to rehearse
Vigilant love-makings. Borders drawn or redrawn.
Drifts and siltings. All the brokerage of years.
A few strides apace and how far we travel.

Gull

An oilslick, jetsam of a tanker under
a flag of convenience and here's another
wing filmy and sealed, that waddle
of shame on the rocks a grounded gull
wide-eyed as a girl tarred and feathered.

Remember 'foe' and 'Erin' and 'liberty'?
The birds did whistle and sweetly sing
Changing their notes from tree to tree
The song they sang was old Ireland free.
Our innocence still a bird on the wing.

Who are we now? Our daily conspiracy
of mood and idioms, delta of memories,
names and quarrels of a shared place,
frail rootedness, complicities of ease,
womb of overlaps and shifting boundaries.

The rocks keep crumbling, trapping soil
in pioneer decays of lichen and moss;
some water-plant is netting in its root
the silt that clots a slobland. What
bird will nest its dream in our humus?

Sing the darker musics of complexity.

Image

Eighty miles or so from where I write
A divided house in love with an old hate
Feuds and kills. A ghostly tit for tat.
Bitter scores no one settles outright.

Even the terms are alien: 'Prod and Teague'.
Who are you neutral for and who against?
'Tar and featherings', 'kneecap punishments'.
Violence draws frontiers of a golden age.

World of black or white and perfect borders.
Verona or Belfast. It's brother on brother
In worlds long chequered into one another.
An X smeared on a wall. Evacuation orders.

Eighty miles I can't pretend to understand.
On screen tonight a woman mourns a childhood
Lover refound in middle age. Teague and Prod.
Eighty miles from here and still my island.

But I'm no Pilate. I can't now wash my hands,
For I too want these souring wounds to heal.
Those names! Drumshiel, Carn tSiadhail, Loch Shiel.
I'm mapped into landscapes of northern lands.

A woman's image is flying in the face of hate.
The lusts of eye for eye and blow for blow.
Somewhere let Capulet weep for fallen Romeo.
My Teague's hand reaches over a broken Juliet.

Parting

'I think of you often.' He nods
Knowingly. Parting he hugs me, pauses,
Then blurts 'alone in the woods
I've often seen
Your spirit darting among the spruces'.

I wanted to tell him before the train
Drew out how that morning I'd despaired
A wing rapped my window-pane,
A vehemence of friendship
Reaching out. And I wished I'd dared.

Radiance

Think of a black womb of nothingness.
An endless density. Then, it bursts.

A universe scatters through infinity.
The held momentum. The paced gravity.

As the helix tangles and grows complex,
Our feverish sun is a purse that leaks.

A knife-edge between chaos and leap.
Our running down and our building up.

At mutant rims, in my heart of confusion,
Some new and daring jumps of evolution.

Poem of becoming. Dance of detours.
Boundaries fall and a radiance endures.

The red giants die to zinc and carbon.
I grow with ashes of stars in my bone.

Music

Music, always music. And when the violins tumble
a thief has entered me.
Come and gone.
A sneaking anarchy
leaving spoors of memories I never had.

Incognito. Whimpers through crevices and pores,
quick bowings of a violin,
furious *pizzicato*
of what hasn't been
whinnies and hops beyond a future I imagine.

My vigilance breaks down. Rupture of being.
This syncopation. Offbeat,
out of phase
with myself, I vibrate.
What's this breathlessness I can't catch up with?

That flight of thirds mincing up a treble
clef. Lines of joy.
Matrix of frontiers.
EVERY GOOD BOY
DESERVES FAVOUR. Silences are spelling FACE.

Endless glory of some muteness that eludes me.
Approach of another face,
tremelo of forsakenness
naked and homeless.
How can I fold and suckle all its orphanhood?

Music, always music. Neighbour, are you the face
of that thief breaking in,
hollowing me out?
A tumbling violin
breathes its cries in me. I'm womb and mother.

Meditations

1 *After Niels Bohr*

Something in our nature enjoys twin truth.
An electron's double life: in turn a particle
And billow of guesses, waves of the probable.
Neither the one nor the other. World of both.

A thought in flows of the possible takes flesh.
Old Plato's lovely dream, undated and open;
The gain and shortfall of things as they happen.
Love's aims and journeys complement and mesh.

2 *After Alain Aspect*

Two quantums of light are shot contrariwise.
Then, pin one down travelling whatever line –
Already the other moves right-angled to its twin.
Separate togetherness. More a joy than surprise

As though the core knows what nothing has proved.
Unimaginable wholeness. A twitch in a filigree
Shimmers and ripples across a fragile city.
Of course, I still belong to anyone I've loved.

3 *After Werner Heisenberg*

Twin truths. And yet I can never gauge both.
Fix a particle and we've missed its impetus,
Fix its momentum and its place will elude us.
Every bid to fix catches us all in its truth.

Creation delights in this play of peekaboo.
I try to measure your nearness. You abscond.
Your gaze folds me into its infinite beyond.
Fugitive. Ungraspable. I can only love you.

The Bulldog O'Donnell

Chorus of tables and declensions. *Mensa, mensa.*
Latin or arithmetic. Both he'd made us sing
Aloud, his ruler slapping out a rhythm and pace.
Self-reliant and certain of gender and case.
'A sound mind in a sound body.' *Mens sana...*
Bulldog O'Donnell seemed so sure of everything.

Ah, the shattered self. How we'll fall to doubt.
Such tables turned, a temple tumbling down.
Our words. Our gender. Suspicion in commonplace.
Mistrust. Fragmentation. Irony's roundabout.
That long bony finger in the accusative case.
And who am I? All the whitened faces of a clown.

All my shed skins. But I hear him growing hoarse
With his questions: *What's the nominative in Latin?*
Who speaks? Who does what? Whose is the story?
Who's responsible for what? His own mandatory
Reply leading the choir: *The subject, of course!*
I ponder again the swish and metre of his baton.

My foibles, my moods, my myths. Even the sham.
For all that, I still weave a fragile city
Of trust. Blame me, friend. Praise me more.
What's best in me is what you love me for.
Our gazes intersect. And yes, here I am
So inconsistent, yet someone is counting on me.

Amo, amas, amat... He is pointing fingers
At himself, at me, at a neighbour. His chant
of boundaries: first, second and third person.
Conjugations of love. Was he really so certain?
That huge foot slamming the floor, a cincture's
Swayed scansion: *amamus, amatis, amant.*

FEAST

You must sit down, sayes Love, and taste my meat:
So I did sit and eat.

GEORGE HERBERT

Abundance

(for Marie)

To be there, childlike, when it happens.
Nothing I've ever earned or achieved.
Delight. Sudden quivers of abundance.

A whole glorious day with a friend.
Brunch. This honeyed bread. Talk.
All the time in the world to spend.

Those icy stings and a gladdened vein,
an autumn swim tingling my nape,
dousing pleasure on a sleepy brain.

Watching children on a bandstand floor;
some irrepressible urge to celebrate,
squealing, tramping, pleading for more.

November birches with leaves of apricot.
After a long walk in the frosty air,
to warm our palms around a coffee-pot.

Waves and moments of energy released.
I hoard them. A child with sweets and cakes
chortles at prospects of a midnight feast.

So much is that might never have been.

Pond

We'd been netting minnows in the pond all morning.
I knew he was palling with a boy from the avenue
I'd never liked. I still hear my jealous warning:
'If you play with him, then I won't play with you.'

Today a friend greeted me with a fleeting kiss,
Which seemed to glance traces of moments spun
To hours of lovemaking. Is it that I've known bliss?
That riddle of one in many, many in the one.

I remember how he'd smiled and didn't say a thing,
Just idly tossed a pebble to the middle of the pond.
Its plump and sucking fall expanded ring by ring.
A fiesta of hoops keeps swelling beyond and beyond.

Tight-Wire

Strolling fields behind the tent I glance
Figures leaving glares of light.
Wild applause inside.
Elephants to dance;
Now the acrobats delight
Children, now the juggling clown.
Someone hands a faded dressing gown.
Steadied, out she'll stride

Over guy-wires, over littered mud and cans
Past an empty pony stall
Slipping in among
Hung-out clothes and vans.
There she'll seem too small and frail.
No one saw who stepped the wire.
Those who clap her clap their own desire.
Someone always young

Slinging ropes between two garden sheds
Full of reckless festive grace
Seems to dare to flout
Endless overheads
Nothing underwrites but space.
Thrills of business just for fun
Touch the dreams of things we might have done.
Steadied, she'll step out.

Wireless

The word 'certain' and deep down I remember
a late-night newsreader's somnolent timbre
signing off just before the National Anthem.

A cabinet wireless square and solid as a world
around us, that row of knobs I'd once twirled
to eavesdrop on crackles and exotic noises

Riding the empty air. An innocence unravelled.
So much of what was certain a dominance veiled.
Suddenly it's a world multiple and bewildering

As foreign rumours and echoes we couldn't gag
when the tuning needle meandered over Europe:
Berlin, Stockholm, Paris, Hilversum, Prague.

Traces of static. An opulence breaking in.
I've grown to love the grit of interference.
Sizz and hubbub. So many cities of conversation.

Still a longing for the certain and overall.
To reach for timeless skies if only to fall
again into the deeper moments of what's ours.

Radio-waves vault to an overlayer and bounce.
A search for order in one man's resonance;
lives hueing and colouring the words we share.

Coherence hinted. A wager. Something guessed.
Echo of echo. Traces. Rumour of rumour.
This feast at which I'm both host and guest.

Michaelmas at Glendalough

Twin-lake valley scattered with remnants
Of praise and work and damp silence.
A path between the upper and lower lake
Greases with leaves. Is it the heartbreak
Of a season or the still ghosts of prayer
Hiding in birches? There's chill in the air,
Soon these leaves will fossilise in frost.
Something living stiffens and is lost.

Clusters of monks gathered in a first
Burgeoning, that strange lyrical outburst
Of separate worlds just newly spliced:
The lush blackbird, the eastern Christ.
I sense one watching from his beehive hut
As the upper lake gleams its sudden cross-cut
Of sunlight and epiphany and the lower lake
Clouds with all that's ordinary and opaque.

He stares. He'll bring his gleam of sun
To Europe after the Visigoth and Hun.
Will it all go so wrong? The dominance,
A loss of boundaries and shades of nuance.
Somehow everything's distant and mediated
The sacred blurs. Too veiled. Too weighted.
He's staring at an ideal. Let his face
Turn back to the shadows of the commonplace.

The lower lake darkens towards October.
He gazes. The waters are deep and sober.
Freedom and dignity, a love of the profane;
Some Luther is hallowing the ordinary again.
The best when spoilt will soon be worse:
Roundhead and votary of sweet commerce,
Then soiler and technocrat, a male caged
By a reason too controlled and disengaged.

Old ghosts of desire stir the undergrowth;
Two worlds and we crave the best of both
On this greasy path between two cisterns.
Michaelmas at Glendalough as a century turns.
My feastday. The air fills with fragility,
The choices and wounds of double polity.
Now in the shadows, now in the sun;
Can angels of this heart and mind be one?

Leisure

What does it mean?
Suddenly, effortlessly, to touch the core.
Mostly in the glow of friends
but today just strolling the length of a city street.
Carnival moments.
The apple back on its tree
in a garden lost, a garden longed for.

I move among traders.
Stacks of aubergines, rows of tiger-lilies.
Rings of silver and cornelian.
A feast of action.
Crosslegged, an Indian plays
music on a saw-blade glittering in the sun.

In the sweat of thy face
shalt thou eat bread. First hearing
that story, I'd bled for Adam.
I bump into an acquaintance and begin to apologise.
'Taking a break,
Be hard at it tomorrow'
Puritan me, so afraid of paradise.

Anaxagoras the sage
(a century before Plato) mulled it over
on a street like this in Athens.
First question: *Why are you here on earth?*
Answer: *To behold.*
No excuses called for.
Contemplation. Seeing. Fierce and intense.

This majesty. This fullness.
Does it all foreshadow another Eden?
The air is laden with yearning.
I can't say for what and I can't be silent either.
Rejoice. Rejoice.
To attest the gift of a day.
To saunter and gaze. To own the world.

Invitation

Anywhere and always just as you expect it least,
Welling or oozing from nowhere a desire to feast.

At Auschwitz Wolf hums Brahms' rhapsody by heart
As Eddy, thief turned juggler, rehearses his art.

Fling and abandon, gaieties colourful and porous.
The Mexican beggar's skirt, an Araner's *crios*.

Irresistible laughter, hiss and giggle of overflow.
That Black engine-driver crooning his life's motto:

'Paint or tell a story, sing or shovel coal,
You gotta get a glory or the job lacks soul.'

Abundance of joy bubbling some underground jazz.
A voice whispers: Be with me tonight in paradise.

Celebration

Once our days were years. Now years are days.
A guest glances a clock on a kitchen shelf
As though he'd suddenly woken from a daze:
It's gone so fast I must have enjoyed myself.

The tiniest ticks in glacial ages of stones
Or even less on crueller scales of stars;
A man with dreams of past and future zones
Loses a self in aeons of clocks and calendars.

Lines with loops of days or months or years.
We don't know how to begin to think of time:
Memory, expectation, our shy hopes and fears –
Easier to word the taste of mango with lime.

Which Native American people used to say:
We never come to time, it comes to us?
Unwind the clock and let it come as it may,
Turn or spiral, a plot thickening and viscous.

But image on image seems to return to one:
A medium in which our doings move, a continuity
Inscribed and cumulative, all done or undone
A chain of traces across a fragile city.

Delicate filigree. Tables of face-to-faceness,
Years of talk and laughter's shooting star.
The healing moment mango and lime caress.
To choose to say we're glad we've come so far.

Expectation

Waiting for you it's all those years ago,
Flutters of courtship smile in your approach.
Is it the gypsy earrings, the enamelled broach,
Native amber beads I'd brought from Chicago?

Doublespeak of dress that hides and flirts.
Little hoists of ceremony: tilts of a cap,
Hints of calves fattening over an ankle strap.
A giddiness of feasting gathers in dusky skirts.

Delight

Let the meal be simple. A big plate
of mussels, warm bread with garlic,
and enough mulled wine to celebrate

Being here. I open a hinged mussel
pincering a balloon of plump meat
from the blue angel wings of a shell.

A table's rising decibels of fun.
Such gossip. A story caps a story.
Banter. Then, another pun on a pun.

Iced yoghurt snipes at my temples.
My tongue matches a strawberry's heart
with its rough skin of goose-pimples.

Conversations fragment. Tête-à-tête,
a confidence passes between two guests.
A munch of oatcake thickens my palate.

Juicy fumes of a mango on my breath.
(A poem with no end but delight.)
I knife to the oblong host of its pith.

Wine sinks its ease to the nerve-ends.
Here are my roots. I feast on faces.
Boundless laughter. A radiance of friends.

Courtesy

1

I bring my basketful to serve
Our table. Everything mine is yours.
Everything. Without reserve.

Poems to which I still revert.
Gauguin. Matisse. Renoir's pear-shaped women.
Music I've heard. Blessed Schubert.

Ecstasies I'll never understand –
Mandelstam's instants of splendour, the world
A plain apple in his hand.

Lost faces. Those whose heirs
I was. My print-out of their genes,
Seed and breed of forbears.

Whatever I've become – courtesy
Of lovers, friends or friends of friends.
All those traces in me.

The living and dead. My sum
Of being. A host open and woundable.
Here I am!

2

Tiny as a firefly under the night sky,
We try to imagine stars that travel
Two million light years to reach the eye.

Long ago on a stormy and starless night
Old people used keep a half-door opened,
Anyone passing could make for the light.

The Russian astronauts leaving after them
Bread and salt for the next to dock
At the station. Small symbols of welcome.

Who's that outsider waiting for you?
We try to imagine how destinies unravel
Across the years towards their rendezvous.

A space for wanderers, lone or dispossessed.
At this table we've laid one empty place,
That old courtesy for the missing guest.

3

Never again just this.
Once-off. Ongoing wistfulness.
Wine loosening through my thighs.
Closeness. Our sudden huddle of intimacy.
These hours we're citizens of paradise.

A nourishment of senses.
Such fierce delight tenses
Between affections and the moments
When, like a theatre after its applause,
This house will fall again to silence.

Let gaieties outweigh
Their own misgivings. Emigré
And native, my desire attends
The moment in and out of time
Which even when it ceases never ends.

I feed on such courtesy.
These guests keep countenancing me.
Mine always mine. This complicity
Of faces, companions, breadbreakers.
You and you and you. My fragile city.

Dance

1 *Weaving*

So tables aside! Any dance at all.
I'd loved our flight from the formal.
Our broken observance. Rock and Roll.
The Twist. Disco. Sweet and manic,
Our blare of rapture. Alone. Freelance.
But I yearn again for ritual, organic
Patterns, circlings, the whorled dance.

Sweated repetitiveness of reels that grew
To their ecstasy. A shrug. Yelped *yeoo*.
Quadrilles without the high buckled shoe,
Ribboned wigs, swallow-tailed elegance
Of Napoleon's court or Paris ballroom,
Figures needling an embroidery of dance,
Chaine-de-dames. Fan and perfume.

More a passionate sameness than grace.
Hospitality. Feelings of inclusiveness
As we lined up there. Face to face.
Expectant. Keats's lovers in the gaze
Of a moment but ready to step it out
Across the swollen belly of a vase.
Tableaux of memory wake in that shout:

Take the floor! The first batoned tone
Of a *céilí* band. *The Mason's Apron,
Humours of Bandon. The Bridge of Athlone.*
A swing. A turn. The skipping march.
Limerick's Walls, The Siege of Ennis.
Side-step and stoop under the arch.
Our linked arms. A scent of dizziness.

Openness. Again and again to realign.
Another face and the moves must begin
Anew. And we unfold into our design.
I want to dance for ever. A veil
Shakes between now-ness and infinity.
Touch of hands. Communal and frail.
Our courtesies weave a fragile city.

2 *Play*

Is music a love-making? To dance in rhythm,
our bodies sharing these humours and fancies.

Low-necks. Just glimmers of beautiful limbs.
The changing and same ballet of intimacies.

Yet all that talk of 'playing with fire'.
The puritans have put us through our paces.

Dante's lustful shades were doing time
relearning for eternity swift embraces.

This arm around my waist. That shoulder
leaning on mine the freight of its histories.

Blouses. Men with cummerbunds. The gleam
and sizzle of dresses. To glorify what is.

No matter what this dance will be here.
Blessed be its weavings and its intricacies.

O fragile city of my trust and desire!
Our glancings. No longer any need to possess.

Tiny dalliances. Middle ground of playfulness.
This dance shuffling our warmth as we pass.

3 *Glimpse*

A few are sitting this one out: spectators,
Thinkers on the outside, catching a glance
Of how the dancers turn like Plato's stars.

Dance in a cosmos, cosmos in the light of dance.
An ancient image, I know, stuff of visionaries:
Harmony, music of spheres, the mystic's trance.

The whirl of it! Barefaced and fluid boundaries,
I'm watching through a window, sipping iced beer
In the night air. Ripe images. Old quandaries.

To dance between infinites of quark and star,
Lost in a labyrinth we ourselves have planned.
Detached and involved. Half-god, half-creature.

Glimpse from a stillness beyond rhythm's command.
An inner stillness in the shifting views of dancers.
To stand under heavens you can never understand.

Rhythm of now. Now the beat.
Forever. Forever.
Our *qui vive* of listening feet.
Sweetest seizure.

Such ecstasies as maddened Corybants:
A *bodhrán*'s crescendo,
Frenzy of bones knuckling the dance,
High wire of let-go.

A reel with all its plans. Drumbeat,
Steps or turns,
Stubborn ritual. Some dizzy heat
Of spirit yearns.

Forever. Forever. How to remember
In each move and pose,
Even the music's pitch and timbre
Crave repose?

Leaps in an infinite womb. I yield.
The dance's yes
Teeters on the rim of Achilles' shield.
Vertigo of gladness.

Index of titles and first lines

(Titles are in italics, first lines in roman type.)